Richard III's North

People & Places Around

the Northern Dales

Edited by Kim Harding

Forward by Philippa Langley MBE

©Kim Harding 2017

ISBN 978-0-9935970-7-7

Printed by Mosaic Print & Design
Moor Edge, Snaisgill, Middleton-in-Teesdale,
County Durham DL12 0RP
mosaic@mooredge.co.uk
www.mosaicteesdale.co.uk

Disclaimer
All websites, admission information and contact details are correct at the time of printing but may be subject to change.

Acknowledgements:
Northern Dales Richard III Group logo (Allan Jones)

Richard Duke of Gloucester (chancel arch) and St Anthony effigy (St Mary's Barnard Castle PCC)

Members of the NDRIIIG who contributed to the research, photographs and writing of this guidebook

Bill Hare (Bedale Historical Society)

Photo of Ravensworth Castle: Maggie Boyd

Photo of Snape Castle: Gillian Smith

Photos of Middleham Castle, Skipton Castle, Holy Trinity Skipton: Karen Lewis

Photo of St Helen & Holy Cross, Sheriff Hutton: Karen Griebling

Photos of Holy Trinity Kendal, St Andrew's Penrith, Holy Trinity & St Constantine Wetheral, Brougham Castle, Shap Abbey, Bewcastle: Andrew Judson

Photograph of Jervaulx Abbey reproduced with kind permission of the Burdon Family

Photographs taken at Barnard Castle, Brougham Castle, Carlisle Castle, Easby Abbey, Egglestone Abbey, Middleham Castle, Pickering Castle, Richmond Castle and Shap Abbey reproduced by kind permission of English Heritage

*In memory of Beverley Holland (1944-2014),
ever loyal to Richard and the North*

Loyaulte nous lie

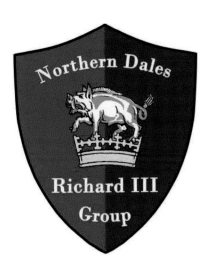

Contents

Foreword 7

Introduction...9

Richard of Gloucester and the North 11

DURHAM & NORTHUMBERLAND..13

1. Barnard Castle 13

2. Egglestone Abbey 18

3. Cotherstone Castle 19

4. Bowes & Streatlam 20

5. Gainford & Selaby..21

6. Walworth Castle 23

7. Staindrop 23

8. Raby Castle 25

9. Witton Castle 27

10. Tudhoe 28

11. Low Butterby Farm (Beautrove) & Croxdale Hall 28

12. Brancepeth Castle..30

13. Bearpark 32

14. Durham Cathedral, Durham...33

15. Chester-le-Street & Lumley Castle 35

16. Hexham & Simonburn 37

CUMBRIA 39

17. Appleby-in-Westmorland 39

18. Great Musgrave 41

19. Penrith Castle & St Andrew's Church..41

20. Brougham Castle 42

21. Shap Abbey...43

22. Holy Trinity & St Constantine's Church, Wetheral 44

23. Holy Trinity Church, Kendal 45

24. Carlisle Cathedral & Castle; Bewcastle...47

NORTH YORKSHIRE 50

25.   Croft-on-Tees..50

26.   Ravensworth Castle 52

27.   Sedbury Hall & St Agatha's Church, Gilling West 53

28.   St Mary's Church, South Cowton 55

29.   Richmond Castle & Marrick Priory..57

30.   Easby Abbey, Richmond & St Agatha's Church...................................59

31.   St Anne's Church, Catterick...60

32.   Hornby Castle & St Mary's Church..62

33.   Castle Bolton 64

34.   Nappa Hall & St Oswald's Church, Askrigg 66

35.   St Andrew's Church, Aysgarth..68

36.   Holy Trinity Church, Wensley...69

37.   Coverham Abbey & Holy Trinity Church..70

38.   Middleham Castle & St Mary & St Alkelda's Church...........................72

39.   Jervaulx Abbey...77

40.   Bedale & St Gregory's Church, ...79

41.   Snape Castle 81

42.   Masham...82

43.   West Tanfield 84

44.   Norton Conyers & St Mary's Church, Wath...85

45.   Ripon Cathedral , Fountains Abbey & Markenfield Hall 86

46.   Skipton Castle & Holy Trinity Church 89

47.   Scotton & Knaresborough..91

48.   St Martin's Church, Allerton Mauleverer 92

49.   Cock Lodge, Topcliffe..93

50.   Upsall Castle & St Wilfrid's Church, South Kilvington..........................94

51.   Helmsley & Pickering 95

52.   Sheriff Hutton 98

53.   Scarborough & Scarborough Castle 101

Foreword

Richard III is one of England's best-known kings, a fame recently increased by the dig and discovery of his remains in Greyfriars, Leicester undertaken by the Looking for Richard project led by myself. Up and down the country many groups of local enthusiasts and historians still seek to discover more about the real Richard, his life and times, and here in the north of England, where Richard spent the majority of his teenage and adult life, there are strong Ricardian connections around every corner. As his brother's viceroy and then as king, Richard made strong alliances here, forming bonds of loyalty to and from the nobility across the northern counties, and shaping the landscape physically and culturally during his rule. I commend the Northern Dales RIII Group for this excellent guide to the region which demonstrates the range of fifteenth century locations here and the importance of Richard and his northern alliances, when Duke of Gloucester and King of England.

Philippa Langley MBE

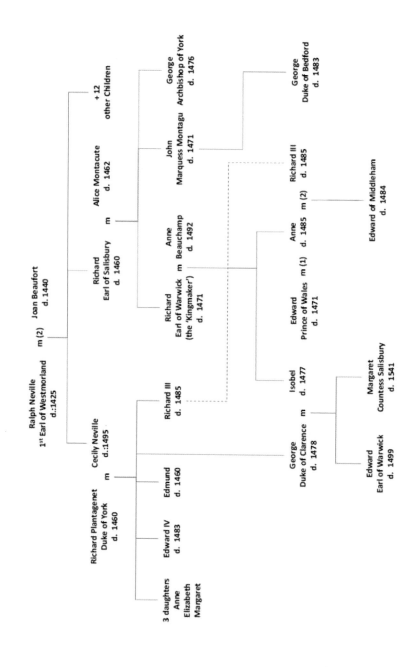

Introduction

The Northern Dales Richard III Group was founded in 2013 in Barnard Castle after the timely discovery of the lost remains of Richard III in August 2012. Fresh interest and enthusiasm combined with well-established local Richard III connections drew together long-standing Ricardians as well as those newly fascinated by the recent events. Our informal group meets every 4-6 weeks in Barnard Castle to study aspects of late C15th history with particular focus on the reign and reputation of Richard III and his local links. Members attend from across Teesdale and Swaledale, Darlington and district, and as far as Northallerton and Northumberland.

In 2013 co-chair Beverley Holland was keen that the group promote Richard's especial connection with the Barnard Castle area and the north of England but also that it help connect people with the medieval era, its people and personalities, events and places. Members have now collaborated to create this guidebook to 'King Richard's North': a busy but non-exhaustive array of interesting places to see, places to visit or places to note as you drive past, with details of their Ricardian or late C15th connections. Whilst the city of York itself was Richard's 'fair citie', his local capital and key to his lordship in the North, it is already well-documented for visitors in an excellent and extensive webpage by the Yorkshire Branch of the Richard III Society and so we warmly commend visitors to this: http://www.richardiiiyorkshire.org/historic_york.html

Not all locations in this guide are open to the public and we ask that the owners' privacy be respected.

Richard of Gloucester and the North

Richard III is unique in being England's only 'Northern' king. Born at Fotheringhay (Northants.) he spent his early years there, in London and at Ludlow on the Welsh Marches, but from age 12 until his death aged 32 Richard was primarily connected with and resident in the North: from his knightly training in the households of Richard Neville, Earl of Warwick, to his key northern residences as a married man at Middleham, Barnard Castle, and Sheriff Hutton. His lordship of a wide range of castles and estates across Yorkshire, Cumberland, Westmorland and County Durham added to his political roles in the North, as High Sheriff of Cumberland; Lieutenant of the North & Commander-in-Chief against the Scots; Warden of the West Marches and President of the Council of the North. His command of the Anglo-Scottish wars from 1480 to 1482 included the final return of Berwick to English rule. As 'lord of the North' Richard gained a strong and loyal following but also was an advocate for the economic prosperity of an under-represented region, bringing tax concessions, improving townships and in the case of Scarborough creating a new shire incorporate.

Richard also engaged religiously with the North, favouring the northern saints Ninian of Whithorn and Cuthbert of Durham, and he planned a number of religious foundations here, principally at Middleham, Barnard Castle and York Minster, as well as with gifts to local churches, chapelries and monastic foundations. His legacy did not dissipate – as late as the middle of the C20th, well over a third of the men in Coverdale (near Middleham) were still named Richard. Even now Sir Francis Bacon's words of 1622 might be said to still hold true: in the North "... *the memory of King Richard was so strong, that it lay like lees in the bottom of men's hearts; and if the vessel was but stirred it would come up....*"

DURHAM & NORTHUMBERLAND

1. Barnard Castle [DL12 8NE]

Although the rights of possession were long disputed by the Bishops of Durham, Richard, Duke of Gloucester acquired the Lordship of Barnard Castle by parliamentary act in 1474 through his marriage to the Earl of Warwick's daughter, Anne, receiving it as a portion of her mother's estates. As Lord of Barnard Castle he spent a significant amount of time and money here in the late 1470s and early 1480s. His boar badge can be seen on several buildings, including the castle and church where his sculpted head can be seen. The unique number of these physical signs of his connection to the town indicate his strong attachment here. The Lordship extends from Forest-in-Teesdale as far as Gainford, approximately 40 miles alongside the River Tees. Richard also gained the Lordship of Richmond by 1478, giving him an unbroken power-base from Barnard Castle across Swaledale and into Wensleydale. Whilst the Lordship yielded only one third the income of Middleham, Richard was in residence here in the later 1470s and in 1480. After becoming King Richard had little time to spend in Barnard Castle but on his northern itinerary in early May 1484, travelling from Nottingham to Newcastle, he paid his last visit to Barnard Castle.

Castle [DL12 8PR] - Richard Neville, Earl of Warwick, previous owner of the castle, had the wardship of Richard of Gloucester, who may well have first visited Barnard Castle during knightly training in his early teens, hunting in the Marwood estate which extends north-west from the castle. As Lord of Barnard Castle Richard of Gloucester conducted extensive and stylish improvements: he rebuilt the Mortham Tower and dwellings for grooms, whilst the north-east Brackenbury Tower may have gained its name after the trusted local Yorkist affiliate, Robert Brackenbury of Gainford and Selaby.

Richard's symbolic boar – now heavily eroded – is carved in the ceiling of the Great Chamber above its oriel mullioned window.

In 1478 Richard gained permission for a licence to found and endow a Collegiate Chapel within the Chapel of St Margaret in the castle grounds, for a Dean and twelve priests, ten clerks, and six choristers, (twice the size of the College intended for Middleham) to the honour of Christ Jesus, the Virgin Mary, St Margaret and St Ninian. It would serve as a perpetual chantry, offering prayers for the souls of Richard, the King and Queen, his brothers and sisters, his father, wife and son, and would have been the most significant late medieval chantry in Co. Durham. However, although some masonry suggests work may have begun on the College, it was never completed.

Richard drew some of his most faithful associates from Barnard Castle and the locality – Fitzhugh, Brackenbury, Bowes, Ratcliffe - and appointed several of his retainers here. In 1474 Richard Ratcliffe became Chief Forester of Teesdale and Steward of the Castle, a post formerly held by Ralph Neville of Raby. Miles Forrest was Groom of the Wardrobe until his death in 1484. Thomases Thursby, Merley and Metcalfe, variously Yeomen of the King's Chamber, Sergeant-at-Arms and Auditor were here during Richard's kingship.

English Heritage: open daily Apr-Oct (Sat/Sun only Nov-Mar); admission charge.

Town & Museum - Richard's boar badge forms part of the town heraldic arms and is etched in stone in the miniature golf course close to the Castle's gateway.

Gloucester Place is named after Richard, and just outside St Mary's Church a small garden area dedicated to his memory bears a blue plaque. The residential nursing home 'King's Court' on the Marketplace, formerly the King's Head inn, is the location of the original gateway into the castle grounds: all of the properties on the west side of The Bank and Marketplace face rearward onto the Outer Ward of the Castle.

Another Ricardian boar can be seen in the Bowes Museum [DL12 8NP] on Newgate - a large sculpted facing stone which once graced a building opposite St Mary's Church, possibly connected with Richard's intended Collegiate foundation. Sadly, a stone once known to be in Thorngate with the name *'Richardus'*, *'cut in a most beautifully raised letter'*, is now lost. In the mid-C19th a house on Newgate still contained an ancient oaken chair, conjectured to have been part of the castle furniture during Richard's Lordship. The crown of England was positioned at both the centre of the cross-rail and on the foot-rail, but this antique is also lost.

The Bowes Museum is open daily 10-5; admission charge.

Blagraves House - The ancient house now called Blagraves (on the left descending The Bank) was given by Richard in 1484 to Joan, widow of Miles Forrest (Keeper of the King's Wardrobe) and her son, possibly as an act of thanks for services rendered to Richard's mother (Forrest was a former servant of Cecily Neville). One Henry Forrest, servant at Middleham, may have been a son. Forrest along with John Dighton  was put in the frame by Thomas More for the supposed murder of Edward IV's sons. On one of the exterior walls of Blagraves is a stone 'boar passant', the badge of Richard III, and in the early C16th Blagraves was a public house known as 'The Boar's Head'. Remains of a medieval hunting lodge which may also have been gifted to the Forrest family stand on private land north of the town. Blagraves is a private residence currently operating as a restaurant. See website for opening times.

St Mary's Church - Richard was a generous benefactor of St Mary's and the C15th alterations show an imaginative awareness of the needs of the building. From 1477-1485 Richard's contribution of 40 marks [approx. £20,000 today] provided widened north and south aisles, a north porch, a vestry with a chamber above for a priest, and a clerestory level of windows in the nave alongside a decorated chancel arch and a staircase to serve a new rood loft.

Chancel arch with Richard's portrait head: Edward IV's crowned head (left) is rather stylised, possibly suggesting that the stonemason had never met the King. Richard (right) is wearing his ducal coronet and his far more individual face, with distinctive chin and wavy hair, may indicate a 'from life' portrayal of his features.

St Anthony (north transept): The carved stone sculpture of St. Anthony of Egypt depicts him with his crozier, a bible and supportive flanking boars. Richard was devoted to St. Anthony and it may be that this stone work (once located on Newgate opposite St Mary's) originates from early building work on the College Richard intended, or else formed part of the Augustinian friary at the foot of The Bank.

Late C15th Tees marble font (north transept): This late C15th octagonal font is of black 'marble' from the quarry of nearby Egglestone Abbey. Sculpted with initial letters M, T, A and E, the intermediate sections bear a complex masonic, merchant or guild mark. 'A' and 'E' may refer to Robert Ellerton, Abbot of Egglestone Abbey 1476-95. Its near-identical twin at Holy Trinity Startforth (½ mile south of St Mary's) is possibly dated to 1484 by the initials 'R E' (for 'Robert Ellerton'), and also the initials 'K R', possibly suggestive of its creation during Richard's reign.

Richard's boar badge is carved on the exterior left-hand side of the east window arch of the South Transept.

St Mary's Church is open to visitors during daylight hours.

2. Egglestone Abbey [DL12 9TN]

Egglestone Abbey was founded c. 1198 for a small number of Premonstratensian canons from Easby Abbey (N. Yorks). The Premonstratensians lived communally but did not take monastic vows. Their members were ordained as canons (priests), not monks. As such they had the authority to celebrate mass and administer sacraments, which monks had not. During Richard III's lifetime there was still an abbey community although it remained impoverished throughout its existence. It was ravaged by the Scots in 1315, with further Scots attacks in the C15th. The large black Tees marble tomb sited in the nave is that of Sir Ralph Bowes (1450–1512), who was knighted by Richard of Gloucester in 1482 on the Scots campaign, and created High Sheriff of Durham in Oct 1483, serving 20 years.

Richard would have been aware of Egglestone Abbey. During the reign of his brother Edward IV (1461-70, 1471-83) Richard was appointed President of the new Council of the North in 1472, and as Lord of Barnard Castle and Middleham he led the northern Lords, including the Earls of Northumberland and Westmorland and the Bishop of Durham, in a successful retaliation against Scots forces despoiling northern ecclesiastical sites such as Egglestone Abbey. In responding to the Scots he besieged and captured Berwick-on-Tweed in 1482. Berwick has remained part of England ever since.

The Abbey owned the local river quarry of black 'Tees marble', used for several local medieval fonts, including the late C15th octagonal example at nearby St Mary's, Barnard Castle, on which the sculpted initial letters 'A' and 'E' may refer to Robert Ellerton, Abbot of Egglestone Abbey, 1476-95. The abbey was dissolved by Henry VIII in 1540 and was granted into private hands (Robert Strelley) in 1548. English Heritage: free entry during daylight hours.

3. Cotherstone Castle [DL12 9QW]

A wooden motte and bailey castle (c. 1090) was replaced by a stone edifice in 1200 of which remains an earth mound and traces of a fishpond. Castle stone was re-purposed in local walls and dwellings. The castle was owned in the C15th by the Fitzhughs of Ravensworth.

With no surviving remains of the castle, its location is a Schedule D Ancient Monument field by a small side-road descending to the Rivers Tees and Balder.

4. Bowes & Streatlam

Streatlam & the Bowes family [DL12 8TZ]

The manor of Streatlam came by marriage into the Bowes family and 'Old William' Bowes (1389-1465) rebuilt the castle. The medieval manor was rebuilt in later centuries by the Bowes Lyon family, Earls of Strathmore, as one of their seats alongside Glamis Castle (Angus, Scotland) and Gibside (Northumberland), but was finally demolished in 1959. Streatlam Park - located off the A688 - is in private ownership and is used for equestrian events.

Sir William Bowes (c. 1414-66) married Maud Fitzhugh of Ravensworth. He was at the Rout of Ludford in 1459 and knighted c. 1460, later being appointed Sheriff of Northumberland and Warden of the Middle Marches under John Neville, Marquis Montagu and then Richard of Gloucester. His son William Bowes (d.1474) married the niece of the Bishop of Durham, but died without issue and was succeeded by his brother.

Sir Ralph Bowes (1450–1512) married Margery Conyers, the daughter and co-heir of Sir Richard Conyers of South Cowton, c. 1475. Richard, Duke of Gloucester purchased the advowson of Seaham church from Ralph Bowes in 1476. Ralph became Chief Chamberlain of Durham in 1481, was knighted in 1481 on the Scots campaign and created High Sheriff of Durham in Oct 1483, serving 20 years. He fought for Richard at Bosworth and his black Tees marble tomb is now located at Egglestone Abbey.

Bowes Castle [DL12 9HP]

Bowes Castle was built in the C12th over the remains of the Roman fort of Lavatris, on a strategic route between England and Scotland. During medieval times it was held by the Honour of Richmond and its design was similar to Middleham Castle. Despite huge investment from Henry II, it was subject to Scottish raids and sieges, resulting in ruination by the mid-C14th. Reclaimed by the Crown, it was briefly controlled by the Nevilles between 1444 and 1471, and its C12th keep is extant.

English Heritage: free entry during daylight hours.

5. Gainford & Selaby

St Mary's Church, Gainford [DL2 3EN]

St Mary's is the earliest church in Teesdale, originally dedicated to St Cuthbert and on the site of a pre-Conquest Saxon monastery. It was rebuilt in the C13th and until 1866 was the parent church of St Mary's, Barnard Castle. Outside south of the chancel lies the blue-grey limestone table monument of Sir William Pudsey. The inscription reads: HIC IACEUT DNS WILLMS PUDCEY MILES ET ELIZABETH UXOR EIUS QUORU' AIARU PROPICIETUR DEUS AMEN.

Whilst his older brother Ralph of nearby Barford fought for the Lancastrians (at one point having care of Henry VI after the Battle of Hexham in 1464), Sir William Pudsey, born c. 1414, married Elizabeth Aske c. 1444 and as an indentured retainer of the Earl of Salisbury he was a committed Yorkist. He fought at the Battle of Blore Heath in 1459 and was knighted by 1472.

St Mary's is also the likely resting place of Sir Robert Brackenbury. Formerly a possible retainer of the Earl of Warwick, Brackenbury was a native of nearby Denton and acquired land in Selaby (two miles from Gainford) in 1481 from Sir William Pudsey. He was Treasurer of Richard, Duke of Gloucester's household from 1479, and on Richard's accession was Master of the Mint and Constable of the Tower of London, receiving lands and titles in Essex, Sussex and Kent. He was knighted by Richard III in Dec 1484 and held joint command of the vanguard at Bosworth but died in the battle. Richard III and Robert Brackenbury were the only people in Co. Durham who held lands in the Palatinate which were forfeited under attainder in Henry VII's reign. This attainder was partly reversed in 1489 in favour of Brackenbury's sisters and *"the Bastard Sonne of Sir Robert"*. The will of Richard III's Master of the Rolls - Thomas Barowe – also mentions a bequest of £50 to the son of Robert Brackenbury. Since in 1546 one 'Robert Brakenberie' of Langton, within the parish of Gainford willed that his *'writched and sinfull bodie'* be *'buried within the parish church of Gainforthe besides my father'* – it seems likely that Sir Robert was brought from Bosworth Field for burial at St Mary's. A small brass inscription on the north chancel wall commemorates the burial there of Brackenbury's sister, Katherine and her husband William Pegg.

St Mary's is open to visitors during daylight hours.

Selaby Hall [DL2 3HF]

This residence of Robert Brackenbury is sited on a ridge of Neolithic importance to the north-west of <u>Gainford</u>, with an overview of the village and surrounds. The sole surviving remains of an original C13th building are the stone mullioned walls of the service buildings of the late C18th Georgian mansion erected by the Maude family, now inhabited by a Neville descendant. <u>Selaby Hall is a private residence and not open to the public.</u>

Between Jan 1476 and Dec 1480, in a contract with Elizabeth, widow of the 5th Lord Scrope of <u>Masham</u>, Richard of Gloucester gained the service of her tenants in the village of Winston (west of Gainford).

6. Walworth Castle [DL2 2LY]

Richard Hansard (1455-93) inherited Walworth Manor as its 13th Lord in 1466. He became Constable of <u>Durham</u> Castle c. 1476. Following unrest in the south at Richard III's accession, he was Constable and Steward of Odiham in Hampshire in Dec 1483, with multiple commissions in that county. A castle was built c.1600 on the site of the C12th Walworth Manor, and is now a hotel, open to the public only on National Heritage days.

7. Staindrop [DL2 3NH]

Staindrop was a key town during the reign of the Saxon king Cnut who regarded it as his northern headquarters. Originally designated St Gregory's, the church boasts early Neville memorials in the south aisle, one depicting Euphemia de Clavering, mother of 'Neville's Cross' Ralph Neville. In 1408, Ralph, 1st Earl of Westmorland became the first layman to found a Collegiate Church located a short distance north of St Mary's and at the Dissolution some of its woodwork survived by removal to St Mary's. The Chancel Screen (the only pre-Reformation example in <u>Durham</u>) and the Chancel Stalls with their misericords date to this period. Formerly located in the chancel, Ralph's alabaster tomb (made of marble from the quarries of John of Gaunt at Tutbury) is now sited at the west end, with his effigy and those of his first wife Margaret Stafford (buried in <u>Brancepeth</u>) and second wife Joan Beaufort (buried in Lincoln Cathedral). During the Wars of the Roses the Beaufort Nevilles held the Earldom of Salisbury and of Warwick, and Ralph's grandson Richard was later famous as 'Warwick the Kingmaker' during the reign of Edward IV. Ralph's daughter Cecily (mother of Edward IV and Richard III) was apparently betrothed to Richard, Duke of York at St Mary's Church.

Adjacent to the 1st Earl's tomb is the worn effigy of Margary Neville, second wife of 'Neville's Cross' Ralph, and the sizeable black oak monument to Henry, 5th Earl Westmorland, and his two wives. This is considered one of the finest wooden tombs in northern Europe and bears images of Henry's children in the surrounding niches, carved with the Neville crest and also with the rare inclusion of the 'Neville galley'. Henry's son Charles helped lead the Rising of the North.

The Neville saltire is found widely around the church – in the chancel and C15th nave roof, in stained glass and on the armorial bearings of the early C15th Teesdale font. A knight's medieval helm is perched on a high fixing in the chancel. Chancel sedilia were carved by the same architect as those in Durham Cathedral, and a huge medieval chest with three keyholes stands in the nave, possibly once used to store communion plate in the Collegiate foundation. St Mary's is also known as the last English parish church to celebrate the pre-Reformation mass in Latin.

St Mary's is open to the public during daylight hours.

*Three miles north-west of the village stands Raby Old Lodge, a medieval tower house built for the Nevilles, restored in the C19th and now used privately as holiday accommodation.

8. Raby Castle [DL2 3AH]

Once a Saxon manor house of the Maldred family, Raby Castle passed to the Nevilles in the early C13th when Isabella Neville married Robert FitzMaldred and brought to the marriage her mother's Bulmer inheritance from nearby Brancepeth. Their son Geoffrey adopted the Neville surname and his son acquired by marriage the FitzRanulph estates in Middleham and Coverdale. In 1319 Raby passed to Ralph Neville, later hero of the Battle of Neville's Cross and the first layman to be buried in Durham Cathedral. His son John completed the present castle at Raby (1367-90) and was responsible for the magnificent Neville Screen (1380) in Durham Cathedral. John's son Ralph was created 1st Earl Westmorland, and married as his second wife, Joan Beaufort, daughter of John of Gaunt, Duke of Lancaster. At this time approximately 1000 people lived and worked in Raby Castle. Ralph's youngest daughter Cecily married Richard Plantagenet, Duke of York. Their sons, Edward, Earl of March, and Richard, Duke of Gloucester, became respectively Edward IV and Richard III. Ralph left his wealthy Middleham estates to Cecily's family, the junior branch, and the Raby estates to the family of his first wife Margaret Stafford.

Ralph Neville, 2nd Earl of Westmorland (d. 1484), took little part in the Wars of the Roses, although his younger brother John, Lord Neville, died fighting for Henry VI at the Battle of Towton in 1461. Ralph's nephew, another Ralph, 3rd Earl Westmorland, was created a Knight of the Bath alongside the sons of King Edward IV. In 1477 Ralph 2nd Earl quit all claims to the Neville estates in Yorkshire, ceding them to Richard of Gloucester, who visited Raby in 1478 and twice in 1480. In 1479 Ralph vested Raby and his Durham manors by an 'enfeoffment of use' to his infant great-nephew. Seven of the ten trustees were Richard of Gloucester's adherents.

A justice of the peace in Durham, Ralph 3rd Earl campaigned in Scotland with Richard of Gloucester in 1481-2, and it was to Ralph that Richard sent his urgent request for assistance in June 1483. The

Raby revenues were in Richard III's use from 1483 to Nov 1484 when he granted Ralph manors in Somerset and Berkshire for his 'good services' during the October Rebellion. The 3rd Earl 'fought' on the non-combatant Percy wing at Bosworth. He died and was buried in 1499 at Hornby Castle, Yorkshire, home of his son-in-law, Sir William Conyers.

Richard III's mother Cecily Neville is sometimes described as 'the rose of Raby', although sadly this is a novelistic and lyrical invention of the C18th. Cecily may well have been born in Raby and visited it up to the occasion of her marriage in 1429. A Victorian painting of Cecily can be found in the arcade at the west end of the castle chapel.

The last Neville of Raby took part in the Catholic Rising of the North in 1569 and died penniless in the Low Countries. Raby (and Barnard Castle) were purchased in 1626 by Sir Henry Vane, a member of the royal household, whose family still owns Raby, presently in possession of the 12th Baron Barnard.

Raby Castle and Grounds are open to visitors from Easter to Sept. Please see website for times and prices.

9. Witton Castle [DL14 0DE]

Witton Castle retains few elements of its C15th form after much renovation in the C18th/19th and now lies at the heart of a country holiday and caravan park. The site was originally held by the Crown until the reign of Henry II, when it came into the hands of the Barmpton or Bermeton family in the early C14th. Sir Ralph Eure obtained a licence to crenellate his manor in 1410 and created a three storey tower house with a curtain wall.

Sir Ralph Eure was killed in March 1461 at the Battle of Towton. His son Sir William Eure (1440-pre-1484/1497) married Margaret

Constable, and was Sheriff of Yorkshire in 1482-3. Their son Sir Ralph Eure (1461 - 1539) married Muriel Hastings and was later Sheriff of Northumberland and of Yorkshire. The estate later passed to the Chaytor family of Croft Hall.

Witton Castle is open to guests and residents only.

10. Tudhoe [DL16 6TH]

Tudhoe is first mentioned c. 1200 when Emma de Bulmer of Brancepeth granted the village to Robert FitzMaldred of Raby who had married her daughter Isabella. The lordship continued in the ownership of the Brancepeth/Raby Nevilles. Two Hotons of Tudhoe appear to have fought at Agincourt with Henry V. John Hoton (1454?-85) was a Commissioner of Array for Durham in 1480 to combat the Scots' invasion, serving under Richard of Gloucester. Alongside Richard Hansard of Walworth, Hoton was named as an executor for Sir Ralph Bowes prior to the Scottish campaign of 1482. He accompanied Richard south after the death of Edward IV, and assisted in suppressing the rebellions in the south later in 1483. He was appointed Esquire for the Body to Richard in Dec 1483, and was granted several manors in Hampshire and the role of Constable of Southampton and Christchurch Castles, after which much of his 'work' was in the south. Hoton probably died at Bosworth and was buried in the chapel of Trinity College, Oxford (formerly Durham College).

11. Low Butterby Farm (Beautrove) & Croxdale Hall [DH6 5JP]

The heavily wooded estate of Croxdale Hall (near Sunderland Bridge, Durham) and the nearby estate of Beautrove (now Low Butterby

Farmhouse) were initially owned by the D'Audre family who sold them to the Northumberland Lumley clan in the mid-C13th. In the mid-C16th Christopher Chaytor of Croft married the daughter of Margaret Lumley and Sir John Clervaux of Croft, and so inherited Low Butterby, a moated manor house on a loop of the River Wear. In the late C19th the moat was drained to reveal a skeleton in full C14th chainmail and armour, thought to be a casualty from the skirmishes at nearby Sunderland Bridge prior to the Battle of Neville's Cross (1346). The few medieval remains - moat walls, causeway bridges and some masonry – are incorporated in the current C17th/early C18th estate. The Elizabethan gatehouse was demolished in 1966. A medieval hospital dedicated to St Leonard reputedly stood in an adjoining field where stone coffins and water stoops have been discovered. Low Butterby Farm is privately owned and is not open to the public.

Croxdale came to the Salvin family in 1402 when Gerard Salvin of Harswell, Yorkshire, married Agnes Wharton, heiress of Croxdale and granddaughter to Robert de Whalton, Treasurer of Brittany. Another Gerard Salvin (b. 1448) inherited Croxdale in 1477. He was married to Eleanor Conyers, the daughter of Richard of Gloucester's retainer, Sir Roger Conyers of Wynyard. In an un-dated letter Salvin petitioned Richard to intervene against individuals who, he claimed, had assaulted him at his house, requesting Richard order the Sheriff of the Bishopric of Durham to arrest one Thomas Fishburn. As 'a pore gentilman at my liberte, stou[n]ding to take a maister', Salvin stated he loved 'none so well as yow under God and the king' and offered himself as a retainer to Richard.

A disused C12th chapel in the grounds is a Scheduled Ancient Monument and Grade I listed building. It was used as a Chapel of Ease to St Oswald's Church in Durham until the parish church of St

Bartholomew was built by the Salvins in 1845. The house's medieval and Tudor origins were obscured by major alterations in 1760 and subsequent restorations. Still a family home to the Salvin family, the house is not open to the public although public walking routes nearby allow views of the Hall and Chapel.

12. Brancepeth Castle [DH7 8DF]

Brancepeth Castle was originally founded by the Saxon Bulmers. In 1174 Emma, daughter of the last male heir, Bertram, married Gilbert de Neville, grandson of William I's Admiral of the Fleet. Their daughter Isabella married Robert FitzMaldred of Raby, and their son Geoffrey assumed the surname of Neville in honour of his mother. The Nevilles owned Brancepeth until 1569 when Henry 6th Earl of Westmorland escaped to the continent after the failed Rising of the North, and the property passed to the Crown and thereafter into private hands. Most of the castle was fortified by Ralph, 1st Earl of Westmorland (grandfather of Richard 'Kingmaker' Neville and also of Richard III) in 1397 with two courts, accommodation towers and a moat. It was mostly rebuilt in the C19th with an east gateway and a wall whose projecting towers enclose a courtyard. The site of the deer park is now a golf course.

In a signed letter c.1476 Richard of Gloucester requested the Earl of Westmorland's councillors to settle a 'certain controversy' of farm tenants, possibly from Brancepeth. The Durham councillors included William Claxton, Constable of Brancepeth Castle.

Brancepeth Castle is in private ownership and not generally open to the public; occasionally open for craft fairs/National Heritage days, please check website.

St Brandon's Church, Brancepeth

An early Norman step-stile part built from gravestones, with grating to scrape muddy footwear, stands to the left of the church gates. In a devastating fire of 1998, much of St Brandon's interior was destroyed, with only the Neville Chapel and the two porches surviving intact. Robert Neville's monument and the reconstructed C12th font also survived. Early parts of St Brandon's date from the C12th, with C14th aisles and transepts, and further additions in the late C14th. The following talicised features did not survive the 1998 fire.

The early C15th nave-roof boasted carved corbels including a Neville bull and an angel bearing the Neville arms.

John Cosin, Rector in the 1620s and later Bishop of Durham, installed much woodwork: the altar, pulpit, font cover and high box pews.

An elaborate wooden traceried canopy over the chancel arch lay below a possible rood-loft decorated with the Neville bull, the Stafford knot and other heraldic devices. The lower canopy, possibly once part of the reredos of the Jesus altar in Durham Cathedral, may have been rescued at the Dissolution by George Cliffe, one of Durham's last monks, who became Rector of Brancepeth.

The flat chancel roof with lozenge panels of polished oak depicted angels holding shields and inscriptions. The chancel was fitted with canopied stalls and Elizabethan panelling, and here stood the painted oak effigies (c.1484) from the lost memorial of Ralph Neville (grandfather of Richard III) in full armour and his first wife Margaret Stafford (buried in Brancepeth). A C14th Flemish parish chest was reworked into an altar situated in the Neville Chapel until 1998.

Now sited in the Neville Chapel is the huge stone effigy in full armour with a muzzled bear by his left side, depicting Robert Neville, 'Peacock of the North', who died c. 1319 fighting the Scots at Berwick. Melted roof lead from the 1200°C fire has imparted some yellow glaze to this monument.

The Jesus Chantry was founded by Ralph, 3rd Earl of Westmorland and his wife Isabel in 1483, and endowed with £10 p.a. Two Rectors here were also Abbots of Jervaulx Abbey.

St Brandon's is open to visitors during daylight hours.

13. Bearpark [DH7 7AU]

The medieval estate of Beaurepaire ('beautiful retreat') was created by the Priory and Convent of Durham and its Prior, Bertram de Middleton, in the mid-C13th, as a place to which the monks could easily escape the confines of town along Priors Path, to indulge themselves in recreational pastimes such as fishing and hunting whilst enjoying the panoramic views. The chapel was dedicated to St. Edmund. The Prior owned the lucrative mineral ore pit workings as well as the revenues from coal mined on the 14 farms there. The Priory was extended in 1311 to house 40 monks, and in the early C14th was visited by Kings Edward I, II and III when en route to engagements in Scotland. Standing north of the present village of Bearpark, this residence and hunting park extended to 1300 acres of meadow and arable land, pasture, bog and woodland.

Beaurepaire was damaged in the Scots' approach to Durham in 1315 when they destroyed buildings and *'shote the game'*, before the Battle of Neville's Cross in 1346, but Prior Fossour restored and extended the buildings in the later C14th to be *'lavishly equipped with rich furnishings'*. During the later C15th Prior Richard Bell of Durham (1464-78) was resident here, employing one relative as 'keeper of the park' and another as a mason for further improvements to the manor. He also held 'ludi' ('entertainments') here four times a year. Given Richard's close association with Prior Bell in the 1470s it is likely he visited Beaurepaire. The land was in the ownership of the Chaytors of <u>Witton</u>, prominent local Yorkists at the time.

In 1541 the Estate passed to the Dean and Chapter of Durham following the dissolution of Durham Priory, and Beaurepaire was destroyed by the Scots during the English Civil War with only fragments remaining today. A nearby bridge crossing the River Browney probably dates from the early C15th, and the last colliery on the estate was closed in 1984. A large part of the estate is included in the Neville's Cross battle-site, and the Priory ruins are located on land near to Bearpark Hall Farm.

14. Durham Cathedral, Durham [DH1 3EH]

During the 1460s/70s/80s, the Bishops of Durham were

- Lawrence Booth (1457-76) - buried in Cawood Church
- William Dudley (1476—83) - buried in Westminster Abbey
- John Sherwood (1483—94) – who assisted in the coronation of Richard III, but did not find favour with Henry VII, possibly plotting with Margaret of Burgundy for the Yorkist cause (buried in the English College, Rome).

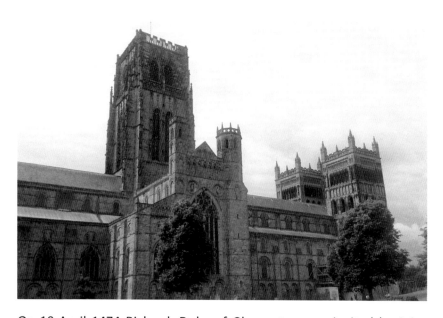

On 10 April 1474 Richard, Duke of Gloucester, was invited by Prior Richard Bell to the confraternity of Durham Priory, and Anne as Duchess was invited to its consorority on 14 Feb 1476. During the 1470s Prior Richard Bell promoted the building of the central tower in Durham Cathedral. As Duke of Gloucester Richard was given hospitality by the monks of Durham on several occasions during the 1470s, visiting the shrine of St Cuthbert in 1479 and mustering troops in the city for war with Scotland in 1480. In July 1482, the cathedral banner of St Cuthbert was carried on Richard's campaign to recapture Berwick. Richard was one of the last monarchs to visit St Cuthbert's Shrine. On St Brendan's Day (16 May) in 1484, after an offering at the High Altar, *'kyng Richard did geve his parlamente Robe of blew vellet wrowght with great Lyons of pure gould a merveilouse rich Cope'*. Until the C16th a choir-screen at the tower crossing displayed a figure of Richard *'all gilted verye beautifull'* amongst statues of other monarchs who were *'devout and godly founders and benefactors'* of Durham Cathedral.

Sir Ralph Neville of Raby, hero of the Battle of Neville's Cross, was the first layman to be buried in Durham Cathedral. His son John (Richard's great-grandfather), also buried here, commissioned the magnificent Neville Screen (1380). Durham Cathedral is open daily; until 6pm Mon-Sat; free entry, with suggested donation £3.

15. Chester-le-Street & Lumley Castle

Church of St. Mary & St. Cuthbert, Chester-le-Street [DH3 3QB]

Initially built of wood to house the body of St Cuthbert transported from Lindisfarne, the church was later stone-built in the C11th with a collegiate foundation created in 1286 by Bishop Bek. In the C15th the north wall was opened with three arches to the Lumley Chapel, removed in the late C16th. The fourteen effigies in the north aisle were installed in 1594 by John, Lord Lumley, to represent his ancestors of which only one may be authentic—the third from the west against the wall, c. 1310-15. Two Lumleys portrayed here were strong Yorkist supporters.

The eleventh effigy, George, 4th Lord Lumley, was knighted by Edward IV. He was joint Constable of Scarborough Castle 1461, Sheriff of Northumberland 1461-3 and 1467-71, Knight of the Shire for Northumberland 1467, Sheriff of Durham and Sedbergh 1471, Joint Keeper with his father of Weardale Forest 1475 and Lord Lieutenant of Northumberland 1480-1. He held a command role in Richard of Gloucester's army at the siege of Berwick in 1482, also entering Edinburgh at the head of the forces, being created Knight Banneret there. A Commissioner of Array in Yorkshire in 1485, he fought for Richard III at Bosworth.

The twelfth effigy, armed and reclining on a helmet, represents Sir Thomas Lumley (1462-87) who married Elizabeth Plantagenet, an illegitimate daughter of Edward IV, in 1477. He was a Justice of the Peace for Durham, and also fought at Bosworth for Richard III.

The C18th North-East historian William Hutchinson notes that a 'book of pedigrees' in the British Museum states that an *'ancient monument or statuary, broken and wasted near the ruins of the chapel in the first ward within the castle called Barnard's castle, was at the honourable means and motion of John Baron Lumley, sent by Sir William Bowes, knight, into this church at Chester [le-Street], to be placed with his ancestors'*. This may be the tenth effigy within the church.

On his visit Hutchinson observed in the churchyard the basin of an old font, *'thrown out and subject to be defaced and spoiled'*, charged with armorial bearings suggesting it was given to the church by George Lord Lumley in the time of Edward IV.

The church is open mornings only during winter months, and mid-am to mid-pm Easter to Oct.

Lumley Castle [DH3 4NX]

Lumley Castle near Chester-le-Street is named for Sir Ralph Lumley, who developed his manor house in 1389 after returning from wars in Scotland. Briefly forfeited owing to Lumley's plotting, the castle was returned to Sir Ralph's grandson, Thomas, in 1421. Appointed Constable of Scarborough Castle for life (jointly with his son) in 1461, Sir Thomas, 2nd Lord Lumley, was involved in the successful siege of Bamburgh Castle and accompanied Edward IV into battle against Margaret of Anjou's forces. He attended Richard's coronation but died in spring 1485 and was succeeded by his son George [see Chester-le-Street]

George's son Thomas (b.1462) married Elizabeth Plantagenet, an illegitimate daughter of Edward IV by his mistress Elizabeth Wayte. Elizabeth Plantagenet died 11 Feb 1503 in Lumley Castle. Thomas fought alongside his father George at Bosworth for Richard III.

Lumley Castle is now a hotel, wedding and conference venue.

16. Hexham & Simonburn

Hexham [NE46 1BA]

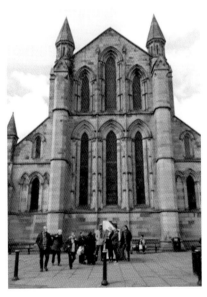

Notable for the Battle of Hexham in May 1464, when John Neville, Marquess Montagu, and his forces fought successfully against the Lancastrians on a site south-east of the town. Local legend maintains that Margaret of Anjou, wife to Lancastrian Henry VI, escaped the battle and was hidden by a worthy local in a place now known as Queen Margaret's Cave; however Margaret was not in England at the time of the battle.

A large number of nobles including Henry Beaufort, 3rd Duke of Somerset, were executed after the Battle of Hexham. Beaufort was captured in a barn at a site now called 'Duke's House', and was beheaded in Hexham marketplace before burial in the Abbey.

Close to Hexham stands the parish of **Simonburn**, known as 'the Great Parish', for which, in 1482, Richard of Gloucester and Anne Neville exchanged the advowson of the parish church of Olney in Buckinghamshire. Following Bosworth, Henry VII seized Richard's possessions including Simonburn, since it was regarded as one of the most valuable livings in the North. It was the largest parish in the diocese of <u>Durham</u>, extending from Hadrian's Wall to Liddesdale in Scotland (33 miles) and covering about 260 square miles. Its C13th church, St Mungo's [NE48 3AW], is open daily to visitors.

CUMBRIA

17. Appleby-in-Westmorland [CA16 6XE]

Thomas Langton of Appleby (1430-1501) was educated at the Carmelite friary here. Later Chaplain to Edward IV c.1476, he helped draft the Royal Household Ordinance in 1478 and as foreign ambassador to Castile, Italy, Burgundy and France, assisted in the marriage treaty of Elizabeth of York and the Dauphin. Elected Bishop of St David's in May 1483, he took part in Richard's coronation, accompanied the King on royal progress and was consecrated Bishop in York on the day before Richard's son's investiture as Prince of Wales. His parish of All Hallows, Gracechurch included the Tower of London and Baynard's Castle, Richard's residence during the Protectorate. He was promoted to Bishop of Salisbury in Feb 1485 and may possibly have been present at Bosworth. His will left monies to the Carmelites, and to maintain a chantry at Appleby for himself, his parents and the faithful deceased there.

Langton's private letter to his friend, the Prior of Christchurch, Canterbury famously mentions Richard:

'He contents the people where he goes best that ever did prince; for many a poor man that hath suffered wrong many days have been relieved and helped by him and his commands in his progress. And in many great cities and towns were great sums of money given him which he hath refused. On my troth I liked never the conditions of any prince so well as his; God hath sent him to us for the weal of us all....'

Appleby Castle, [CA16 6XH] - Whilst its foundations include remains of the Roman fort which protected the local river crossing, Appleby was principally built in the early C12th, with its keep one of the few still intact in England. A defensive stronghold against the Scots, it was royally owned until gifted to the Vieuxpont family in King John's reign, and then came by marriage into the Clifford family for nearly 400 years. In 1454, Thomas, 8th Lord Clifford conducted major building works, reconstructing the Great Hall, kitchen, chapel, Great Chamber and the eastern range, with square towers at either end.

During the Wars of the Roses, the Cliffords declared for Lancaster, and in 1460, after the Battle of Wakefield, John Clifford, 9th Baron, mercilessly executed Edmund, Earl of Rutland, younger brother to the future Yorkist King Edward IV. Clifford died four months later at Edward's victorious Battle of Towton, was attainted (declared traitor) and his lands confiscated. From 1461 to 1485, the Lordship of Westmorland was held by Richard, Duke of Gloucester (later Richard III) and Appleby Castle was probably in the hands of Sir John Parr of Kendal.

Appleby Castle is now a private residence with parts open to the public during summer months for small private tours which can be booked via its website.

18.   Great Musgrave village [CA17 4DW]

This village from which the Musgrave family originated, lies a mile west of Brough. Marrying into the Stapelton family of Edenhall and the Clifford family of Skipton during the reign of Edward IV, the Musgraves were traditionally Keepers of Bewcastle near Carlisle, one of the critical defensive outposts of the Western March on the Scottish border. John and Richard Musgrave were Squires of the Body to Richard III, and served Richard in the south of England in 1484. Edward Musgrave (1461-1542) of Hartley Castle, Kirkby Stephen, married Alice, the sister of Richard Ratcliffe, in 1484. William Musgrave of Penrith fought for Richard III at Bosworth, dying in the battle.

19.   Penrith Castle & St Andrew's Church [CA11 7EA]

Richard of Gloucester was granted the Manor of Penrith in 1471 after the Battle of Barnet, and he may often have stayed at Penrith Castle during his time as Sheriff of Cumberland, using it as a base to counter the Scots. The castle may have been modified during his lordship, with large windows to private apartments, a banqueting hall, and new gatehouse.   English Heritage – free entry during daylight hours.

St. Andrew's Church – in the south aisle a modern window exhibits two fragments of medieval glass, once thought to represent Richard III's parents (Richard and Cecily) but more likely to be his maternal grandparents, Ralph Neville and Joan Beaufort, who were granted Penrith in 1396. At the north-west corner a waterspout still shows the 'bear & ragged staff', cognizance of the Neville family. Open to visitors during daylight hours.

Dockray Hall [CA11 7DE] (formerly The Gloucester Arms) was built as a defensive pele tower by Richard's grandfather Ralph Neville and Richard may have stayed here. A wooden panel of early date in the main bar depicts a possible 'planta genista' (broom pod), and stonework above the main doorway shows Richard's boar badge. Three low-relief wooden panels of post-C15th date depict Richard III, his wife Anne, and his royal arms supported by boars. Now a working pub and restaurant; please see website for opening times.

Richard and John Musgrave of Penrith were esquires of the body to Richard III and two other brothers were retained by him. William Musgrave died at Bosworth alongside Richard III, according to 'The Ballad of Bosworth Field', and the family arms can still be seen in Penrith.

20. Brougham Castle [CA10 2AA]

Brougham Castle stands near the site of the Roman fort of Brocavum. Along with Appleby and Brough it protected the line of communication between Carlisle and Yorkshire. In 1214 the half-barony of Brougham was granted to Robert de Vieuxpont in return for supporting King John. It passed into the hands of the Clifford family in 1269 when Roger Clifford married Isabel de Vieuxpont.

By 1344 the castle was in a state of disrepair following the wars with Scotland and the Cliffords preferred the safer confines of their castle in Skipton. It is likely that Brougham was garrisoned during the Wars of the Roses given its proximity to the Nevilles at Penrith (the Cliffords being Lancastrians). When Edward IV gained the throne in 1461 the lands of John Clifford, 9th Baron, were given to Sir William Parr. A year later Henry Clifford, John's son, was pardoned, and after Bosworth he was granted the return of the family estates by Henry VII. English Heritage: open daily Apr-Oct (Sat/Sun only Nov-Mar); admission charge.

21. Shap Abbey [CA10 3NB]

The remains of this C12th Premonstratensian abbey include a late C15th tower. The last abbey to be founded in England, it was also the last to be dissolved in 1540, with much of its decorated stone used for nearby Lowther Hall. English Heritage – free entry during daylight hours.

The 'monk-bishop' Richard Redman, Abbot of Shap Abbey and Commissary General for the Premonstratensian abbeys in England, was also Bishop of St Asaph's during Richard III's tenure in the North.

He was born in Levens, Westmorland, serving first Edward IV and then Richard III on his council and accompanying Richard during negotiations with the Scots in 1484. He carried the paten holding the Host at Richard's coronation and attended him on progress via Magdalen College, Oxford. He was also present when Bishop Russell of Lincoln presented the Great Seal to Richard at the Angel & Royal Inn in Grantham on 19 October 1483 to issue a death warrant against the Duke of Buckingham. Redman became entangled in the affairs of Lambert Simnel in 1487 but seems to have escaped Tudor censure with promotions to Exeter and then Ely.

22. Holy Trinity & St Constantine's Church, Wetheral [CA4 8HA]

Whilst this church was established in the C16th, it contains the earlier tomb and alabaster effigies of Sir Richard Salkeld (c.1420-1500) of Corby, Cumberland, and his wife Jane Vaux.

Salkeld was a lawyer, Sheriff of Cumberland and retainer of Lord Neville, before being created an esquire of the body for Richard III. As a member of Richard's council, he was sent to negotiate with the Scots in 1484. The church is often locked: contact the Incumbent - (01228) 560332

23. Holy Trinity Church, Kendal [LA9 5AF]

In the Parr Chapel of Holy Trinity, Kendal stands the black marble table tomb of Sir William Parr (1434–83). A stalwart Yorkist, Sir William fought alongside the Earl of Warwick at Banbury in 1469 and was sent by George of Clarence to negotiate with Edward IV for safe conduct and pardons. Sir William joined Edward IV on his return from exile in 1471 and fought at the battles of Barnet and Tewkesbury. He served Edward IV as Comptroller of the Household, sat as knight of the shire for Westmorland in 1467 and 1473, was High Sheriff of

Cumberland for 1473 and invested Knight of the Garter in 1474. He took part in the funeral of Edward IV.

Sir William was married to Elizabeth Fitzhugh of Ravensworth whose mother Alice Neville, was cousin to Edward IV and Richard III. He did not attend Richard's coronation despite being given a position as

canopy bearer, possibly owing to ill-health as he died shortly after. His wife was present as a lady-in-waiting to Queen Anne, a role she fulfilled until Anne's death in 1485. Sir William and Elizabeth were grandparents to Katherine Parr, sixth wife of Henry VIII.

Sir William's father, Sir Thomas (d. 1464), was active for the Yorkists during the Wars of the Roses and briefly attainted in 1459 by the Lancastrian side.

Sir John Parr, brother to Sir William, was an ardent Yorkist, and was made Sheriff of Westmorland for life in 1462. Thomas, another brother to Sir William, was killed at the Battle of Barnet in 1471 fighting in the forces of Richard of Gloucester.

Holy Trinity Church is open to visitors during daylight hours.

24. Carlisle Cathedral & Castle; Bewcastle

Carlisle Cathedral [CA3 8TZ]

Carlisle Cathedral was founded in the C12th as an Augustinian priory and benefitted from renovations funded by Richard, Duke of Gloucester. Bishop Richard Bell (1410-96) was previously Prior of Durham (1464-78). In 1465 Bell attended the lavish enthronement banquet for George Neville, Archbishop of York and he frequently entertained and admitted Richard and Anne, Duke and Duchess of Gloucester, to the Confraternity of Durham Priory in the 1470s. Bell wrote to Anne Neville in April 1477 concerning his nephew Elias, expressing the hope that Richard would accept him into his service as *'hys man'*. By 1478 Richard of Gloucester's patronage secured Bell's elevation to the bishopric of Carlisle. Bell was in attendance on the newly-crowned Richard III as he entered the city of York on 29 August 1483 and was still present a week later when Richard invested his son Edward as Prince of Wales.

The north aisle contains a series of late medieval paintings on the reverse of the choir stalls, resembling the illustrations from a C12th Durham copy of Bede's 'Life of Saint Cuthbert', suggesting that Bishop Bell had borrowed this manuscript. A mermaid with comb and glass on one of the C15th choir misericords also echoes a badge on Durham's central tower, constructed whilst Bell was Prior.

Bell died in 1496. His large brass memorial in the choir (covered by a rug) shows him in full vestments and mitre, holding a bible and his bishop's crozier. A brass fillet around the tomb depicts a fascinating variety of animals – pig, fox, dog, crocodile, bat - and two animals best described as 'sauropod dinosaurs'!

Carlisle Cathedral is open daily 8am-6.15pm (-5pm Sunday); Bishop Bell's memorial is not visible to the public except on request.

Carlisle Castle [CA3 8UR]

Carlisle Castle, constructed in the C11th, was the military base for the Lord Warden of the Marches guarding the Scottish border. The castle's outer gatehouse in the centre of the south curtain wall was built in the late C14th to house the Sheriff of Cumberland and was where he would receive his revenues. Richard of Gloucester was appointed Sheriff of Cumberland for life in February 1475 for which he received fees, the demesne lands of Carlisle Castle and a grant of £40 annually from the citizens of Carlisle. From late 1480-1, Richard obtained a royal grant and supervised repairs to Carlisle's walls. (Rickergate, a principal street leading north from the city centre, is named after Richard.)

In early 1483, just prior to Edward IV's death, Richard was granted in perpetuity a palatine lordship of the West March consisting of Cumberland, Westmorland, and any parts of southwest Scotland he conquered. The castle suffered some damage during the early years of the Wars of the Roses but Richard of Gloucester had the Tile (or Musgrave) Tower, a purpose-built gun tower, rebuilt c.1483 and a weathered red sandstone panel to its right may show Richard's boar badge. On the third storey of the keep a walled recess bears stonework carvings from the 1480s – these include heraldry from local families (Percys and Dacres), religious iconography and a boar signifying the lordship of Richard of Gloucester.

In 1475, Sir William Parr was Gloucester's Lieutenant of Carlisle. Humphrey, Lord Dacre, was later appointed in the 1480s, with William Musgrave exercising the office of Constable of Carlisle Castle by September 1484.

English Heritage: open daily mid-Feb - Oct (Sat/Sun only Nov-mid-Feb); admission charge.

Bewcastle [CA6 6PX]

Edward IV granted the estate and border stronghold of Bewcastle to Richard, Duke of Gloucester in 1478, which Richard retained as King. He improved Bewcastle's basic keep and moat by rebuilding the gatehouse and repairing the walls, and he appointed the Routledges of Bewcastle as his sergeants. An extant letter from Richard to his brother Edward IV explains that the castle is difficult to maintain because of constant border raids. The castle is on private land within Demesne Farm. It can be viewed from a nearby footpath.

NORTH YORKSHIRE

25. Croft-on-Tees [DL2 2SG]

This was formerly the manor of the Clervaux family, who were rewarded after 1066 with lands at Bootham, York. The Scropes of Castle Bolton held Croft until 1464–5, when John le Scrope exchanged all his property in Croft with Sir Richard Clervaux who was esquire of the body to Henry VI. Clervaux's mother was a Lumley and her uncle was Ralph Neville (Richard III's grandfather). In 1477–8 Edward IV granted Sir Richard free warren in the lordships of Croft but this led to a violent dispute with his neighbour, Roland Place of Halnaby, their quarrel extending to the parish church. Clervaux was a retainer of Richard as Duke and part of a Middleham Castle account roll of 1457-60 was used to bind his own family cartulary document (containing family wills and title deeds). He may have gifted a grey horse to Richard III, named for him. Clervaux died in 1490. The last of the family married Christopher Chaytor of Butterby, Durham, surveyor-general in Northumbria for Queen Elizabeth I. The estate remains in the Chaytor family today.

St Peter's Church was principally constructed in the early C14th and in the south aisle enclosed by a C15th oak screen stands the outsize grey marble altar tomb of Richard Clervaux, bearing his arms, badge, motto 'Fortune le veit' and the inscription:

Richard Clervaux, once lord of Croft, lies beneath this marble buried. God have mercy on him. He was a squire of the body of King Henry VI., whom God raised to the stars of the lofty Pole; and of the blood of Edward IV and Richard III, in the third degree the one to the other. Who died A.D. 1490.

The clerestory, lowered chancel roof, tower and porch were added in the C15th. The embattled two-storey tower bears on its south face the arms and initials of Roland Place and Richard Clervaux. In 1478 the two landowners were in serious dispute over their land

boundaries and even their rights over seating in church. Richard of Gloucester arbitrated and ruled that they should fence their land, that if a neighbour's cattle strayed they should be driven home, that no man should poach his neighbour's servants, that Clervaux should not 'hunt, hawke, fische or foule' on Place's land without permission and that they should use the pews assigned to their families – Clervaux on the south side, and Place on the north. This reconciliation resulted in a new church porch where the Clervaux and Place arms originally appeared together.

26. Ravensworth Castle [DL11 7ET]

There may have been a castle at Ravensworth from Norman times although the remaining parts of the castle date from the late C14th, when it belonged to Henry, 1st Baron Fitzhugh. In 1391 he enclosed 200 acres around the castle, creating a park. The Fitzhughs were descended from an illegitimate brother of Earl Alan Rufus, whose son founded Jervaulx Abbey at Fors in 1150, and many Fitzhughs are buried at Jervaulx.

The 5th Baron, Sir Henry Fitzhugh, married Alice Neville, cousin to Edward IV, George of Clarence and Richard III and sister to Richard Neville, 16th Earl of Warwick. This firmly tied Sir Henry to the Yorkist cause. He founded a chantry in the castle chapel in 1467.

Their daughter Anne married Francis, 1st Viscount Lovell, one of the principal supporters of Richard III. Lovell's arms displayed a dog so this is referred to in the doggerel written in 1483 by William Colyngbourne, *'The Cat, the Rat and Lovell the Dog/Rule all England under the hog'*.

On Sir Henry's death in 1472, he was succeeded by his son, Richard Fitzhugh, (1457-87), 6th Baron Fitzhugh of Ravensworth. Sir Richard Fitzhugh fought at Richard III's side at Bosworth. Surviving the battle, he was created Lieutenant of the North by Henry Tudor. He died in Nov 1487 at the age of 30.

In 1483, Lady Alice and her daughter, Elizabeth (who married into the Parr family of Kendal), were appointed by Queen Anne to serve as her ladies-in-waiting. They received presents from King Richard, including expensive fabric for dresses. At Richard and Anne's coronation in 1483, Alice and Elizabeth were two of the seven noble ladies given the honour to ride behind the queen.

The castle was in disrepair by the late C16th, after which much of its stone was removed and used for local buildings, leaving few traces. Surviving remains, including a three-storey tower attached to a gatehouse, are visible on private land.

27.   Sedbury Hall & St Agatha's Church, Gilling West

Sedbury Hall [DL10 5LQ]

Sedbury Hall still includes an early embattled tower of three storeys with apparently medieval trefoiled windows on the west. C15th windows from demolished parts of Sedbury Hall were removed in the C19th to the inner gatehouse of Buckden Manor in Northamptonshire. The south wall bears a shield with Darcy, Aske, Conyers and Neville quarters, and the building is styled similarly to nearby Mortham Tower. A licence to celebrate mass in its chapel was granted to Sedbury in 1463.

Sir Christopher Boynton of Sedbury (d. post-1475) married Agnes Scrope of Castle Bolton, and in 1468 they exchanged lands at Easby for those at Gilling and Sedbury which had originally been held by the Scropes of <u>Masham</u>. Upon widowhood, Agnes married Sir Richard Ratcliffe, Steward of <u>Barnard Castle</u> and closely trusted associate of Richard III. Ratcliffe had been knighted by Edward IV at Tewkesbury and was created Knight Banneret by Richard of Gloucester on his Scottish campaign of 1482. He and Richard were also admitted at the same time in 1477 to the Corpus Christi Guild in York. As King, Richard created Ratcliffe High Sheriff of Westmorland and a Knight of the Garter. A letter between the Abbot of <u>Shap</u> and Prior of St Cuthbert's convent at <u>Durham</u> indicates the '*great rule that [Ratcliffe] beareth under the king's grace in our country*'. Ratcliffe died at Bosworth fighting alongside Richard and is recalled in the famous doggerel rhyme '*The Cat, the Rat and Lovell the Dog/Rule all England under the hog*'. Sedbury Hall is currently a conference and exhibition venue.

St Agatha's Church, Gilling West [DL10 5JN]

The village of Gilling was held by the Lords of Richmond in demesne until the attainder of Richard, Earl of Warwick, and it was granted in 1475 to Richard, Duke of Gloucester.

The west wall of St Agatha's holds the black marble monument of Sir Christopher Boynton's son, Sir Henry, and his wife Isabella Lumley of Ravensworth [North Durham], depicting a knight footed with a roebuck and a lady by a cat. Its original location was above the Boynton vault in the north aisle where a chantry was established to pray for the deceased.

28. St Mary's Church, South Cowton [DL7 0JB]

Now under the care of the Churches Conservation Trust, St Mary's Church is situated just south of the village of North Cowton, near Scotch Corner. The original chapel, according to Prior Wessington of Durham (1440), was erected to commemorate the temporary resting place of St Cuthbert's remains.

The present church was built between 1450 and 1470 by Sir Richard Conyers (1444–c.1502). The Conyers of Hornby were one of Richmondshire's richest and most powerful families and Richard's father, Christopher, was Steward of Middleham for the Nevilles during the mid-1400s. The manor of South Cowton was granted to Conyers from Richard, Duke of Gloucester, possibly in the early 1480s. Sir Richard built South Cowton Castle near the church, a tower house thought to lie on the site of an earlier medieval manor. South Cowton Castle is now a farmhouse and not open to the public.

The village of South Cowton suffered population decline possibly from poor harvests and its land was further cleared and enclosed by Conyers for agricultural use. Whilst he may not be the same Richard Conyers knighted during Richard of Gloucester's Scottish campaign of 1482, he stood in high favour with Richard III, created an esquire of the royal household and receiving an annuity in 1484.

Above the south wall door of St Mary's chancel are two panels bearing the arms of the Conyers and the Boynton families and a window containing C15th glass also includes the Conyers arms. The octagonal font dates from C15th, as do the choirstalls (with a 'two-faced' carving), the painted chancel arch and rood screen. The barrel-roofed porch supports a priest's room above it, with a Latin inscription *'Pray for the souls of Richard Conyers and his wife Alice'* over the porch doorway. The church also contains three late C15th alabaster effigies which may represent Sir Richard Conyers and his two wives, Alice Wycliffe and Katherine Bowes. Alternatively they may represent his two daughters, Margery and Margaret, and Margaret's husband, Sir Robert Danby of Yafforth, who was killed at the Battle of Bosworth in 1485.

Sir Richard founded a chantry at the church whose priest was to receive eight marks per annum and to pray for the founder and his wife, Alice and after her, *'Sir Raufe Bowes, kt wcb hath marryed my daughter dame Marjory.'* [Ralph Bowes of Streatlam, Durham)

St Mary's Church is open daily, and is accessible along a farm track off the B1263

29. Richmond Castle & Marrick Priory

Richmond Castle [DL10 4QW]

From the 'Honour of Richmond' and its vast estates gifted to Alan Rufus by William the Conqueror in 1070 as a reward for his savage 'Harrying of the North', Rufus built the great castle overlooking the River Swale. The military strength of the C12th square keep protected the town which arose in the outer bailey of the castle.

The Richmond Earldom was occasionally briefly divided from the Honour but by the later C15th both title and honour had passed to Henry Tudor. Edward IV confiscated the title and granted the Honour to his brother George of Clarence. Upon George's death in 1478, the Honour passed to Richard of Gloucester who had already been granted the Richmondshire estates by Edward IV in 1471.

English Heritage: open daily April-Oct (Sun/Sun only Nov-Mar); admission charge.

Friar's Wynd forms part of a medieval gateway from the inner town to Friary Gardens [DL10 4UJ] where only a bell tower remains of the C15th development of the Franciscan friary established in 1257/8 on land granted by Ralph FitzRandal, <u>Lord of Middleham</u>. In May 1484 Richard III signed a warrant paying 12 marks to the friars of Richmond, *'for the saying of one thousand masses for the soul of King Edward IV'*.

Marrick Priory [DL11 7LD]

Agnes Scrope Boynton Ratcliffe entered this C12th Benedictine priory c.1496. Sister to John, 5th Lord Scrope of Castle Bolton, and a supporter of Richard III, Agnes' second marriage was to Sir Richard Ratcliffe, close friend and advisor of Richard III, who died at Bosworth with the king. Agnes was the only woman named in 50 pardons granted in 1486 by Henry VII. She was active in supporting the Yorkist 'Lambert Simnel' uprising of 1486/7 but later 'took the veil' becoming a vowess, a pragmatic step enabling her to avoid a forced marriage, continue an independent life and manage her possessions. She ran the family estate and holdings, arranged her

son's marriage and attended Corpus Christi celebrations in York in 1498, before retiring to Marrick Priory. On her death she left her father's copy of The Pilgrimage of the Soul to the priory.

The C13th tower remains, along with the chancel ruins and window tracery. Marrick Priory is an Outdoor Education and Residential Centre and is not open to the public.

30. Easby Abbey, Richmond & St Agatha's Church

Easby Abbey, Richmond [DL10 7EU]

Easby is one of the best preserved monasteries of the Premonstratensian 'white canons', with the magnificent refectory, gatehouse and canons' dormitory remaining. Dating from 1152, and sustained by sheep farming, Easby Abbey founded a daughter house in 1198 - Egglestone Abbey in Teesdale. As patrons from the C14th, members of the Scrope family from Castle Bolton were buried at Easby. Between 1478 and 1500 the abbey received regular visitations from Richard Redman, Abbot of Shap and Principal of the Premonstratensians in England. In 1482 Redman found that one John Nym had absconded from the community, charged with improper relations with a widow. Later proven innocent, Nym became Prior of the abbey by 1494.

The abbey was suppressed in 1536, culpable by association with the Pilgrimage of Grace uprising, and within two years most of its buildings had been stripped and demolished. After suppression, an early C16th rood screen was removed to Holy Trinity, Wensley; a bell and eight stalls with canopies were moved to St Mary's Church, Richmond. They bear a device indicating they were installed under Robert Bampton, last Abbot of Easby, 1511–36. An inscription on the south canopy reads in Latin: *'There are ten abuses of the cloister: a refined way of life, delicate food, gossip in the cloister, quarrelling in the chapter, discord in the choir, negligent pupils, disobedience of youth, stubbornness of age, obstinacy of the monks.'*

English Heritage: open daily 10am-6pm (Apr to Oct); 10am-4pm (Nov-Mar); free entry.

St Agatha's Church, Easby, Richmond [DL10 7EU]

St Agatha's, which uniquely lies within the monastic precincts of Easby, is of early Norman date on a Saxon foundation and boasts a rare fragment of late C12th stained glass, alongside equally rare medieval wall paintings dated c.1250. The paintings, earlier than those in St Peter's, Pickering, show scenes from the Old Testament on the north wall, including the Garden of Eden, and stories from the New Testament on the south wall. The church also contains a copy of the Easby Cross, a copy of a carved apostolic pillar dated 790CE (the original resides in the V&A Museum), an early Romanesque font and examples of arrow-sharpening grooves on the church door jambs. The church is open to visitors during daylight hours.

31.   St Anne's Church, Catterick [DL10 7LN]

During the 1470s the Manor of Catterick was in the possession of George of Clarence and after his execution in 1478, it was granted in 1484 to Sir John Conyers for life. It was later returned to George of Clarence's daughter, Margaret, Countess of Salisbury.

St Anne's Church was built from 1412, an enterprise contracted by Katherine, wife of John Burgh, William Burgh her son and Richard of Cracall (Crakehall near Bedale). The brasses of William Burgh (d.1442) and his son William (d.1462) are located in the north aisle. The chantry 'porch' of St. James was added c.1491 for another William Burgh who died in 1492, and his wife Elizabeth Conyers and their brass is located on a wall-mounted panel. The tower and south porch are both C15th, and also the octagonal font, which bears shields with the arms of Burgh, Fitzhugh, Scrope, Dacre, Darcy and Neville, and the inscription 'CLAR FON' (clear fountain).

William Burgh (d. 1492) fought for Richard Neville, Earl of Warwick, at the Battle of Edgecote in 1469 but was later an indentured retainer of Richard of Gloucester, by virtue of his brother-in-law, Sir John Conyers, who was Steward and Constable of Middleham Castle.

St Anne's Church is open to the public during daylight hours.

32. Hornby Castle & St Mary's Church

Hornby Castle [DL8 1NQ]

Hornby Castle was built as a tower house in the late C14th by the St Quentin family. Although the tower is extant, the principal remains are C16th, renovated in the C18th. Sir Christopher Conyers (1393–1462/5), whose family had married into the St Quentins, served the Nevilles and the house of York. He was bailiff of the Honour of Richmond in 1436 during the Earl of Salisbury's tenure, and in 1464 was commissioned alongside the Earl of Warwick and Lords Greystoke and Fitzhugh to retrieve three key Northumbrian castles held by the Lancastrians.

Christopher's son, Sir John Conyers, was Sheriff of Yorkshire, Constable and Steward of Middleham, Bailiff and Steward of Richmond, as well as a Knight of the Garter. He fought for the Yorkists at the battles of Blore Heath, Northampton and Towton but also sided with Warwick's rebellion, raising Wensleydale men  for 'Robin of Redesdale' and the Battle of Edgecote in 1469. After 1471 he was a Justice of the Peace for the North Riding, and later a loyal retainer and probable ducal councillor of Richard, Duke of Gloucester, who made him a Knight of the Body. Sir John carried the sceptre during Richard's coronation and was later installed as Warden of the East March of Scotland. He fought for Richard at Bosworth and survived, although his youngest son, William, also fought and was killed.

A carved reference to Sir John in the oriel window sill of the Hornby Tower survived until the 1930s when several ancient pieces of demolished masonry were sold to the Burrell Collection in Glasgow.

Sir John's secretary, Master John Harrington - from a junior line of the Lancashire Harringtons and also nephew to Sir William Parr of Kendal – was a Cambridge graduate and favoured legal notary of Richard III. He was Chief Justice to the Church Courts in York, the legal agent and registrar of William Poteman (one of Richard's most preferred clerical protégés). He was also clerk to the Royal Council by the end of 1483 and custodian of the records of Richard's Collegiate foundation of chantry priests at York.

Of the C14th fortified manor the south range and tower still survive alongside remnants of a rectangular courtyard indicating the dual military and domestic functions of the castle. Granted a licence to crenellate in 1284, the roof was gabled with ornamented windows below. The castle later passed from the Conyers family in the mid-Tudor period to the Earls of Holderness and then the Dukes of Leeds.

Hornby Castle is a private residence and not open to visitors.

St. Mary's Church, Hornby [DL8 1NH]

St Mary's, Hornby was built c. 1080 on the site of an earlier Saxon church. The upper level of the tower was added in the late C15th and contains a bell given by Sir William Conyers (1468-1524). The south chapel's late C15th parclose screen is painted with birds, flowers and foliage and there is original C14th glass in the north aisle east window. The church houses several brass, alabaster and stone effigies and monuments: a knight and his lady, possibly the builder of the south aisle, Sir John Conyers and his wife, Margaret St Quintin, a black ledger stone with brass figures of Thomas Mountford (d.1489) and his family, and another ledger with empty matrices for the brasses of Christopher Conyers and Ellen Rolleston, his wife.

Anne, daughter of Ralph Neville, 3rd Earl Westmorland, was married to Sir William Conyers. The Earl died at Hornby Castle in 1499 and is buried in St Mary's, Hornby. He was created Knight of the Bath alongside the two sons of Edward IV, and was strongly supportive of Richard of Gloucester's tenure of the north and demesnes in County Durham. It was to Ralph Neville that Richard sent his urgent letter of 13 June 1483, asking for assistance regarding a plot against his life.

33.   Castle Bolton [DL8 4ET]

Castle Bolton overlooks the valley of Wensleydale. Licence to crenellate was granted to Sir Richard Scrope, Chancellor of England, in 1379 and building was completed in 1399.

Richard, 3rd Lord Scrope was a ward of Ralph Neville, Earl of Westmorland and married Margaret Neville, the sister of Cecily (Richard III's mother). His grandson John (b.1437) became 5th Baron Scrope in 1459. A Knight of the Garter, he was committed to the Yorkist cause, fighting at Northampton and suffering *'sore hurt'* at the Battle of Towton. Henry VI reputedly stayed briefly at Castle Bolton after the Battle of <u>Hexham</u> (1464), and Scrope supported Richard Neville, Earl of Warwick, in his 1469 rebellion against Edward IV. He took part in the 1475 'French invasion' and in the Scottish campaign of 1481-2. He served on Richard III's Council, and fought at Bosworth, surviving to later support the Lambert Simnel uprising. Imprisoned and fined, he was restricted to residency in the south of England until his death in 1498.

Castle Bolton is open to visitors: Apr-Oct 10am-5pm. Occasional falconry and re-enactment displays (please check website).

34. Nappa Hall & St Oswald's Church, Askrigg

Nappa Hall [DL8 3JZ]

Nappa Hall is one of the best examples of a fortified manor house in the north of England and the ancestral home of the Metcalfe family. It was built by Sir James Metcalfe in 1459 on land given by the Scropes of Castle Bolton for Metcalfe's valour at Agincourt. His son Thomas continued its development in the early 1470s. Sir James also founded the chantry of St Anne in St Oswald's Church, Askrigg in 1467.

Two towers stood at either side of a grand hall, with a minstrels' gallery. A single-storey hall sits between a four-storey crenellated western tower and a two-storey eastern tower. For a time Nappa's warrens (such as at Lady Hill) supplied silver sable rabbit skins to the Russian royal family and aristocracy.

Sir James' son Thomas Metcalfe (1424-1504) was a Privy Councillor in 1460. As the Chancellor of the Duchy of Lancaster (July 1483 - Sept 1486), he was a trusted member of Richard III's Council and judge of the Duchy court that sat at Westminster. In 1485-6 he received a grant of the office of Surveyor of the Castle and Lordship of Middleham, and of all manors and lordships within the liberty of Richmond. He fought for Richard III at Bosworth.

Miles Metcalfe (1428-86), Thomas' younger brother, was a lawyer, Recorder of York and Justice of Assize at Lancaster. In 1470 Miles and his wife Matilda became members of the York Corpus Christi Guild. He was appointed as Attorney General to the Lordship of Middleham. In 1477/8, 1482 and 1484 he represented the City of York in Parliament. He was also King's Deputy at the Council of the Duchy of Lancaster and a member of Richard's Ducal Council and the King's Council of the North. After Bosworth Miles continued as

Recorder despite attempts by Henry VII to have him removed from the post. Both he and Thomas were exempted from the pardon Henry VII granted to the northern counties. Dying in 1486 in a room above Monk Bar (York), Miles is buried in York Minster.

Sir James Metcalfe (1460–1539) (son of Thomas) served on the Scottish border under Richard, Duke of Gloucester and held the post of Coroner of the Marshalsea of the King's Household. He was also Master Forester of Wensleydale, Raydale and Bishopdale.

Descendants of the Metcalfe family lived at Nappa Hall until the early C21st; the house is now privately owned and not open to the public.

St Oswald's Church, Askrigg [DL8 3HT]

The site of St Oswald's has been used for Christian worship since before 1180, and was originally a chapel-of-ease for Aysgarth. The Cistercians who founded Fors Abbey (1 mile west of Askrigg) later removed to found Jervaulx but retained many estates around the village. The present church dates from c.1466, and includes the

C15th barrel-vaulted nave roof and a possibly pre-C15th font. The south aisle chantry to St Anne was founded by Sir James Metcalfe of Nappa Hall in 1467, for prayers *'for the good estate of the King and Queen, of himself and his sons, and their souls...'* Askrigg was exempt from the 'forest law' which covered the hunting grounds of the dale, so became a useful trading hub for the upper dale in the medieval period.

35.   St Andrew's Church, Aysgarth [DL8 3SR]

St Andrew's (rebuilt 1536) possesses the stunning carved and decorated rood screen and abbot's stall which were brought to the church at the Dissolution of Jervaulx Abbey and the execution of Abbot Adam Sedbergh after the Pilgrimage of Grace. Local legend claims that twenty men carried it from Jervaulx across Witton Moor to Aysgarth, a church owned by the abbey. The brightly-coloured and gilded rood-screen formerly stood between the chancel and nave but now adjoins the Lady Chapel

The screen is decorated with bright foliage and fruit and depicts antelopes, elephants-and-castles and miniature devils, indicators of the human capacity for sin. The barrel (tun) also carved on the screen was the rebus (logo) of William de Heslington who became Abbot at Jervaulx in 1472, indicating that the rood screen was commissioned during his tenure. The abbot's stall, also brought from Jervaulx, includes the same rebus 'hazel-tun' on its poppy-headed bench-end. Other detailed carving on the stall includes a monkey, a medieval-style lion and a fantastical animal. A wooden beam above the vestry door, inscribed to Abbot Adam Sedbergh of Jervaulx, is said to commemorate the rebuilding of St Andrew's in 1536.

The church is open to visitors during daylight hours.

36. Holy Trinity Church, Wensley [DL8 4HY]

Holy Trinity dates from the mid-C13th, with C14th/C15th alterations. The benched south porch dates from the C15th and the north porch from the C14th, with arms above. Early C20th restoration uncovered fragments of medieval wall paintings (1300), including the figures of Jacob and Esau and St Eloi. A wooden reliquary of St Agatha is dated to the early C15th. The chancel contains a late C14th brass of priest Simon of Wensley, a memorial to members of the Scrope family and early C16th choir stalls carved with heraldic animals. The tower arch frames a C15th choir screen. On the north side of the nave is the Scrope family pew, partly constructed of the carved parclose screen moved from Easby Abbey at the Dissolution. In the east window of the south aisle are fragments of medieval stained glass.

The church is irregularly open to visitors; please contact the Vicar - (01969) 663097

37. Coverham Abbey & Holy Trinity Church

Coverham Abbey [DL8 4RL]

A Premonstratensian monastery founded at Swainby (near Northallerton) in 1190 by Helewisia, daughter of the Lord Chief Justice, Ranulf de Glanville, was refounded at Coverham in about 1212 by her son Ranulf FitzRalph, who removed Helewisia's remains to Coverham's chapter house.

Records indicate the abbey was badly damaged in a Scottish raid of 1331, but was rebuilt by the close of the C14th, with fifteen monks and an Abbot in residence. The abbey was dissolved in 1536, its grounds sold, and it quickly became ruinous. A range of monastic buildings, including the abbot's lodging, was retained or re-developed as private dwellings in later centuries, incorporating elements of the abbey architecture. The gatehouse is still partially intact, as are two nave arches, with a rear arch of the gatehouse passage still standing. Other sculptural remains are preserved in private gardens of the residences, including two stone effigies of knights considered to be the sons of the founder, Helewisia, or early lords of Middleham. Ralph Neville, 1st Baron Neville of Raby and father of 'Neville's Cross' Ralph Neville, was buried in Coverham Abbey in 1331.

As the most local abbey to Middleham Castle, it is one of the possible locations for the burial of Edward of Middleham, Richard III's only legitimate son, who died in late April 1484. In 1476 the Abbot appealed to the Bishop of Durham that, their revenues daily decreasing, the monastery was impoverished to the point of degradation and possible abandonment. As Ralph Bowes had recently sold the advowson of the church living of Seaham to Richard of Gloucester, the Abbot appealed to the Bishop for Seaham's revenues to sustain Coverham's income, and Richard duly in turn gave the advowson to the abbey to assist its continued existence. Coverham Abbey was then responsible for supplying Seaham with a monk in priestly orders. An account of the lordship of Middleham's expenses of September 1483 details a visit by the 'lord prince' (Edward of Middleham) who made offerings at Coverham Abbey. Richard also obtained the manor of Coverdale in 1475.

The site is privately owned and not generally open to the public but can be glimpsed from the churchyard of Holy Trinity Church, Coverham. It is currently open once a year for charity under the National Gardens Scheme.

Holy Trinity Church, Coverham [DL8 4HX]

Holy Trinity is under the care of the Churches Conservation Trust and dates from the C13th. The south aisle was constructed in the C14th and the west tower in the C15th. A lintel over the inner south doorway re-uses a cross shaft dating from the Anglo-Saxon period. The south aisle contains painted glass shields, possibly dating from the medieval period. As King, Richard gave £20 for the repair of Holy Trinity – *'And forsomoche as we of our grace especialle have graunted unto oure trusty and welbelovede in god Thabbot & Convent of Coverham xxli of money towardes the belding theire Churche and reperacione of other things necessarie within thaire place...we therefore wolle & charge you to content & pay unto the said Abbot & Convent the said somme...'* - Richard III, 1484.

38.   Middleham Castle & St Mary & St Alkelda's Church
Middleham Castle [DL8 4QG]

Middleham's first 'motte and bailey' castle stood on William Hill, 400 metres to the southwest of the present castle. In the late C12th Robert FitzRanulph built the stone keep of the new castle - one of the largest in England - and in 1270 Middleham passed by marriage to the Nevilles, successive Lords enlarging and improving the castle. Richard Neville, Earl of Salisbury, a key early Yorkist, inherited Middleham as his chief residence in 1440. After his death at the Battle of Wakefield (1460), his sons Richard, Earl of Warwick, and John, Marquis Montagu also played significant roles during the Wars of the Roses. In August 1461 Edward IV stayed at Middleham for several days and in 1464 defeated Lancastrians were executed at the castle. However, in 1469 Warwick turned against Edward IV and Edward was imprisoned at Middleham that August. The castle was forfeit to the crown in 1471 when Warwick was killed at the Battle of Barnet.

As a ward of the Earl of Warwick, Richard, Duke of Gloucester may well have spent the years of his knightly training in Warwick's northern castles, including Middleham, and may have first met his future wife, Anne Neville, there. His 1461 Commission of Array for the North Parts and Warwick's 1465 grant of 1,000 pounds for his maintenance may suggest Richard was in Warwick's household for some or all of his early teenage years until 1468.

Following Warwick's death, Richard married Warwick's daughter Anne in Jan/Feb 1473 and became Lord of Middleham, one of his chief residences whilst ruling the North on behalf of his brother. His only legitimate son, Edward, was *'borne yn the castell of mydlam'* and died there in late April 1484. The room where he died is still known as the Prince's Chamber and is in the Round Tower at the south-west corner.

Gloucester made Sir John Conyers of Hornby Steward and Constable of Middleham in 1471 and authorised renovations to the castle. In June 1473, Gloucester's retainer, Sir James Tyrell, escorted Anne Beauchamp, widowed Countess of Warwick, from sanctuary in

Beaulieu, Hampshire, to Middleham. The Silesian ambassador Nicolas von Poppelau, visited Richard III at Middleham during early May 1484. This was Richard's last visit to the castle.

The castle contains a variety of interesting sites including a first storey aspect of the Great Hall, a ruined latrine block and evidence of 'bridges' linking the keep to the outer courtyard dwellings. A weathered carved stone to the left of a cupboard in the guard-niche alongside the stairs to the first level of the keep may depict Richard's boar. A replica of the Middleham Jewel is on display in the castle shop. A controversial statue of Richard III by artist Linda Thompson stands to the south of the keep. With a boar at his feet, Richard wears a collar of Yorkist suns but a fantastical basilisk surmounts his back, indicating both Richard's scoliosis and the monstrous reputation levelled at him.

English Heritage: open daily 10-5pm Apr-Oct (Sat/Sun only Nov-Mar); admission charge.

Town In the upper marketplace stands a double flight of steps surmounted by a recumbent stone animal, possibly a bear (Warwick's badge) or a boar (Richard III's badge).

In 1478, Edward IV granted a licence to John Cartmel to found a chantry of Our Lady in the church of Middleham Hospital with a Chapel of Jesus. The hospital was at the east end of the town and the area still named "Chapel Fields" is now occupied by stables.

Middleham Boar Badge – a copper alloy boar badge of Richard III, possibly a gift to one of his retainers, was found in the north moat of Middleham Castle.

Middleham Jewel - this unique late C15th jewel, now in the Yorkshire Museum, was found near Middleham in 1985. Possible owners include Anne Beauchamp, Countess of Warwick, or Anne Neville, Richard III's wife. The gold lozenge-shaped clasp embellished with a sapphire is engraved with the Holy Trinity, a Nativity scene, and fifteen saints in miniature. It is etched with the words of the Agnus Dei and *'tetragrammaton ananizapta'*, a votive to ward off illness.

Middleham Plaque – a copper-alloy disc found at Middleham bearing the initials 'R' and 'A' surrounded by the French motto *'A Vo Plaisir'* (For your pleasure) may be a casket mark given by Richard to his wife Anne.

St Mary & St. Alkelda's Church, Middleham [DL8 4PQ]

Dating from 1280, the church was enlarged in 1340. The decorated Saxon stone near the choir marks the burial of St. Alkelda, a Christian Saxon princess. In 1470 Edward IV granted a licence to John Cartmel, a former Rector, to found a Chantry of Our Lady here which formed the east portion of the south aisle and part of the choir.

In 1477 Richard of Gloucester obtained a licence for 'erecting the church at Middleham into a College' with a Dean, six chaplains, four clerks, a sacristan and six choristers, to offer perpetual masses for the souls of the Yorkist royal family, at a cost of 200 marks. William Beverley became its first Dean. In 1482 a Papal Bull proclaimed in Middleham church in the presence of the Abbots of Jervaulx, St. Mary's, York and Fountains Abbey, confirmed its Statutes. The canons' stalls were dedicated to Richard's favoured saints: Katherine, Barbara, George, Anthony, Cuthbert and Ninian, the latter four celebrated on their feast-days. In 1483 the church became known as the King's College, Middleham. The chantry was closed in 1547 by Act of Parliament but the church remained a Royal Peculiar, laid out in collegiate fashion until the C18th, this status being extinguished in 1845 by a further Act of Parliament.

On the north front of the tower inside the vestry, stands the gravestone of Robert Thornton, 22nd Abbot of Jervaulx and Dean of Middleham, brought from Jervaulx Abbey. It shows thorn leaves and a tun (barrel) as a rebus of his surname and includes an inscription.

In a niche on the west wall is a replica of the Middleham Jewel.

At the western end of the south aisle a window presented in 1934 by the Richard III Society shows Richard, Anne Neville and their son. An altar cloth bearing the arms of Richard and Anne is used on a number of days through the year, and pews bear Ricardian-themed hassocks.

St Mary & St Alkelda's is open to visitors during daylight hours.

39. Jervaulx Abbey [HG4 4PH]

Jervaulx Abbey is a large privately owned Cistercian Abbey set in parkland three miles to the south-east of Middleham. The community was originally founded in 1146 at an exposed site in Fors near Askrigg by the nephew of Earl Alan Rufus of Richmond, and re-established in 1154 at Jervaulx where it became wealthy and famed for sheep-rearing, horse breeding and cheese-making (possibly the first 'Wensleydale' cheese).

Jervaulx was closed in 1537. The last abbot, Adam Sedbergh, who had joined the Pilgrimage of Grace opposing the Dissolution of the monasteries, was hanged. The buildings were stripped of lead and all other valuables and demolished. Too heavy to transport during winter, its lead was buried, and thereafter forgotten. It was later uncovered and used for the re-roofing of York Minster after its disastrous fire of 1984.

Key areas of the church and monastic buildings remain, and the chancel screen and some of the monks' stalls can now be seen in St Andrew's, Aysgarth. The Lady Chapel to the rear of the sanctuary contains a number of stone coffins, the north transept contains a stone altar with consecration crosses and at the central crossing lies the worn stone effigy of Ralph FitzHenry (c. 1280) with medieval grave covers nearby. The abbey was the last resting place of a number of members of the Neville family and the Fitzhughs of Ravensworth.

One of the books in Richard's possession and signed by him 'Richard Gloucestre' was the Fitzhugh Chronicle, written by John Brompton, Abbot of Jervaulx in the early 1450s. William Heslingon was Abbot from 1475 to 1510; and Robert Thornton from 1510 to 1533. Abbot Thornton was buried by the pulpit in St Alkelda's, Middleham where his grave cover stands in the vestry at the west end.

The V&A Museum contains an early C16th black mourning vestment in silk and velvet decorated with the rebus of Robert Thornton and depictions of the Last Judgement worked in silver and silver-gilt thread. There is some speculation that whilst this could be a vestment created for Thornton, it may originally have been a funeral pall. Jervaulx is one of the possible locations for the burial of Richard III's son, Edward of Middleham (d.1484). An anonymous small grave cover lies immediately before the site of the High Altar, suggesting a high status burial. In a list of Edward of Middleham's household expenses for summer 1483 is mention of a visit to Jervaulx and Edward's gift of twenty pence there. Richard III owned several horses – a great grey, a bay and a white - from the stud at Jervaulx. On 7 June 1487 Francis Viscount Lovell and John de la Pole, 1st Earl of Lincoln, encamped by the Abbey as they gathered forces in the 'Lambert Simnel' Yorkist uprising.

The abbey is privately owned but open to the public during daylight hours with an honesty box.

40. Bedale & St Gregory's Church, Bedale [DL8 1AF]

'Bedale Castle', a fortified manor with parkland, stood southwest of the church on a site now occupied by Bedale Hall, with remains visible until the C19th. Possibly founded by 1305 by Brian FitzAlan, a younger brother of the Earl of Richmond, it was likely crenelated. High Sheriff of Yorkshire and custodian of Scotland from 1297, FitzAlan fought against William Wallace at the Battle of Falkirk and built the 'pele' church tower as a defence against Scots invaders. At his death the manor was divided, half by marriage into the Stapleton family and the other half passing into various hands including Francis Viscount Lovell and into the Peirse family by the mid-C17th. Jane, the younger daughter of Sir Miles Stapleton (d. 1466) married John Hudleston of Millom Castle, who was appointed Sheriff of Cumberland by Richard of Gloucester.

Bedale was Lancastrian in allegiance until Richard Neville and Richard of Gloucester held Middleham and Richard's brother George held Richmond. Francis, Viscount Lovell, (c. 1455/6-87), one of Richard III's closest associates and confidants, came from a Lancastrian family but was married to Anna Fitzhugh of nearby Ravensworth, niece to the Earl of Warwick who gained Lovell's wardship. His knightly training at Middleham/Barnard Castle is where he likely first met Richard of Gloucester. His wardship passed to the Duke of Suffolk after Warwick's death. He would fight his last battle alongside the Duke's son, John de la Pole, at Stoke Field in 1487. At the death of his paternal grandmother, Alice Deincourt, Lovell inherited the family estates including the barony of Bedale. In 1477 one John Thomson of Bedale took part in an enquiry into whether Lovell had had the right to present his brother-in-law, George Fitzhugh, to the living of St Gregory's Bedale.

In 1480, Lovell was appointed a Commissioner of Array for the North Riding of Yorkshire. He recruited for the Scottish campaign and was knighted by Richard at Berwick in 1481. In 1483 he was appointed Viscount Lovell and he carried a Sword of State at Richard's coronation as well as accompanying the royal party on progress. He raised troops for Richard in October 1483 and was on guard on the south coast prior to Bosworth. Post-1485 he helped lead the Yorkist and Lambert Simnel uprisings before his possible death at Stoke Field.

St Gregory's Church, Bedale [DL8 1AF]

Much of the C9th church on this site did not survive the Harrowing of the North although traces remain of the Saxon nave and crypt as well

as early Viking and Saxon grave markers. Endowed to <u>Jervaulx Abbey</u>, the C14th north aisle chantry of Brian de Thornhill contains his effigy. Additions at that time include the multi-storey pele tower designed for refuge from Scots invaders as well as several effigies including the alabaster figure of Brian FitzAlan. Extant wall paintings including a left-handed St George slaying the dragon, the clerestory and the top two levels of the tower were added in the C15th, with one C14th bell said to originate from Jervaulx.

St Gregory's is open to visitors during daylight hours.

41. Snape Castle [DL8 2TJ]

Originally a mid-C13th manor house built by Ralph FitzRanulph, Lord of <u>Middleham</u>, Snape Castle passed to the Nevilles on his daughter's marriage. The Nevilles' elevated status brought improvements in the early C15th, probably by George Neville (younger son of Ralph, 1st Earl of Westmorland) designated Baron Latimer in 1432. During the 1460's Richard Neville, Earl of Warwick, held custody of the Latimer estates (including Snape) because of George Neville's mental incapacity. George's son, Sir Henry, was retained by Warwick but was killed on the eve of the Battle of Edgecote in 1469 and Baron Latimer died the same year.

Henry's young son Richard became a ward of the Archbishop of Canterbury but Warwick appears to have retained custody of him until 1471. During Richard Neville's minority Snape was held by Richard of Gloucester and then, as 2nd Lord Latimer, he was a commander of Henry VII's army at the Battle of Stoke in 1487. Snape Castle has a reputation for being a temporary residence for both Richard of Gloucester's mother, Cecily Neville, and his wife Anne although there is no documentary evidence to support this.

In the C16th Catherine Parr, future wife of Henry VIII, lived at Snape with her second husband John Neville, 3rd Baron Latimer, and the property later came to Thomas Cecil, Lord Burghley, who made extensive alterations. The first-floor chapel at the castle, although heavily restored in Victorian times, was built in the C15th and traces remain of a medieval ceiling painting.

The castle is a private residence and is not open to the public and the undercroft of the chapel is rentable holiday accommodation. Visitors are welcome at the chapel itself, accessed via a footpath from the main road through some of the earlier castle remains.

42.   Masham [HG4 4EF]

Masham's first lords were the Dane Gospatric and Earl Siward but it passed in 1328 from the de Waltons to the Scropes and their two family branches, at Castle Bolton and Masham.

Although Henry Scrope was attainted for treason by Henry V (the 'Southampton Plot'), and the Fitzhughs briefly gained the estates, the Scropes regained them in 1446. Sir Thomas, 5th Baron Scrope was rewarded by Lancastrians after the Battle of Blore Heath (1459), and was in Parliament through the reign of Edward IV until 1472.

Sir Thomas, 6th Lord Scrope was indentured in 1475 aged 15 into the household of Richard of Gloucester to be 'hooly at his Rule and guydyng'. Marrying Elizabeth, the daughter of John Neville, Marquis Montagu and Richard's cousin, in 1477, they lived in Middleham or on the Scrope estates at Upsall. He obtained his lands in 1480, was a Commissioner of Array in Richard's Scottish campaign and knighted by him in 1481. He was an MP Nov 1482-Aug 1492, and was cup-bearer at Richard III's coronation. He was party to the Treaty between Richard and James IV of Scotland in Sept 1484 and fought at Bosworth. He did not attend Henry VII's first Parliament and in April 1486 Mashamshire men were raised locally against the new king. The army of the Yorkist claimant Lambert Simnel with Francis Viscount Lovell and John, 1st Earl of Lincoln gathered at Masham on 8 June 1487, and a request was sent to enter the city of York. With his brother Sir John, Sir Thomas Scrope led the abortive storming of the city of York. Refused entry at Bootham Bar, Thomas later fought Henry VII's forces at Stoke Field in Nottinghamshire. Imprisoned in the Tower of London, he was later released, fined and forbidden to live further than 22 miles from London. He received royal orders in 1492 to join an expedition to France and muster men-at-arms, horsemen and archers but died in 1493, aged just 33.

St Mary's Church contains Anglo-Saxon/Norman remains and the remnant of a C8th cross, and was enlarged in the C14th and C15th (north chapel and porch) by the Scrope family. As a centre of the wool trade, Masham was a 'golden prebend' (given to a canon of York Minster), the wealthiest in medieval England, valued at over £166 in the late C13th (in the same year a prebend in Hereford diocese was valued at a single bundle of hay). Masham was also created a 'Peculier' in the C12th – given independence from its diocese - and the Peculier Court of The Four And Twenty still meets twice a year to propose church wardens and dispose apprentice grants to young people of the parish.

George Neville, brother to the Kingmaker and later Archbishop of York, was given the 'golden prebend' aged only 14. It passed to Roger Radcliffe, Dean of St. Paul's, in 1456. John Sherwood, Archdeacon of Richmond (and later Bishop of Durham), took the prebendary in 1471, and John Blythe, nephew of Thomas Rotherham, Archbishop of York, was installed prebend in 1484.

Although owning all Mashamshire and possessing a fortified tower at Clifton (3m. north), the Scropes chiefly resided at Upsall near Thirsk, and they possessed the family chapel of St Stephen's in York Minster where the 5th Lord Scrope founded a chantry for two priests in 1458.

43.   West Tanfield - 'Marmion Tower' [HG4 5JQ]

West Tanfield Manor was granted a licence to crenellate from Edward II but its sole surviving 'Marmion Tower' was built in the early C15th after the manor had passed into the hands of the Fitzhughs of Ravensworth. The ground floor has a barrel-vaulted roof and the upper storeys contain window seats, ornate oriel windows and fireplaces.

English Heritage: free entry daily 10am-4pm.

St Nicholas's Church, West Tanfield contains the fine armoured monument to Sir John Marmion who died in 1387, and of his wife Elizabeth St. Quintin. The tomb is framed by a wrought iron 'canopy' with candles which would have been lit on special occasions. It is believed to be the only one of its kind in England. The manor passed to Marmion's niece Elizabeth (m. Henry, 3rd Baron Fitzhugh) whose grandson Henry, 5th Lord Fitzhugh married Alice Neville, sister of the Earl of Warwick. Fitzhugh was a close supporter of his brother-in-law, especially Warwick's rebellion against Edward IV. After his death in 1472 his widow Alice is said to have spent much of her time at West Tanfield although it is likely she is buried alongside her husband at Jervaulx Abbey. One legend suggests that she gave refuge at West Tanfield to her son-in-law, Francis Lovell after the Battle of Bosworth. The church is open to visitors during daylight hours.

44. Norton Conyers & St Mary's Church, Wath

Norton Conyers (Wath, nr. Ripon) [HG4 5EQ]

Norton Conyers house is a Grade II listed late medieval fortified manor with Stuart and Georgian additions. The site was originally owned by the Conyers family in the C11th but purchased by the Nortons at the end of the C14th. It was confiscated in 1569 because of the family's role in the Rising of the North. Built in brick with two storeys and a four-bay frontage, the interior is much renovated to a C18th style, echoed by the garden scheme.

The house is thought to be the inspiration for the original Thornfield Hall in Charlotte Bronte's 'Jane Eyre'. Bronte visited in 1839, and a legend of a mentally distressed woman in an attic room is attached to the house. In 2004 a blocked staircase was discovered connecting an attic room to the first floor.

Limited opening only during spring/summer, 2-5pm. See website for details.

St Mary's Church, Wath [HG4 5PG]

The church has long been the burial site for the Norton family and contains the worn brass of Sir John Norton (1460-1520) of Norton Conyers and his wife Margaret Ward. The brass consists of six shields and the symbols of the four Gospel writers. His father, also Sir John Norton (1427-89), was a Commissioner of the Peace and fought for Richard III at Bosworth. He is also buried at St Mary's. The Norton and Pigot families helped fund much of the C15th rebuilding of Ripon Minster where their arms are still evident in the south transept.

The church is open to the public during daylight hours.

45. Ripon Cathedral , Fountains Abbey & Markenfield Hall

Ripon Cathedral/Minster [HG4 1QS]

Ripon was a Neville town during the 1450s/60s, wealthy from the profits of the wool trade and the medieval cloth industry, and the Archbishop of York had a palace there (a single archway remains on Kirkgate Street).

In the 1470s Richard of Gloucester became Lay Steward of the Archbishop of York's Lordship of Ripon, with its valuable income, and so had influence in the land transfers and markets that were held in the area. Richard was also keen to link clergy from York and Ripon, especially the outstanding York Minster cleric William Poteman who became a Canon of Ripon in 1478 and in 1479 Master of St Mary Magdalene's Hospital in the town. Frequently consulted at Middleham on clerical matters and at York Minster, Poteman would have been a key ecclesiastic at events in York during Richard's royal progress visit of Sept 1483.

Ripon Cathedral (formerly Minster) was one of the first stone churches in England, founded in AD 672 under the auspices of St Wilfrid whose Saxon crypt - open to visitors - lies under the nave crossing. In the 1450s the central tower collapsed, destroying choir stalls. Rebuilding in the 1480s included fine misericords in the choir (c.1489/90), similar to those in Beverley Minster, depicting biblical scenes including Jonah and Samson and mythical and realistic animals symbolising virtues and vices. The C15th bishop's stall canopy is now sited above the altar in the Chapel of Justice and Peace.

In the north transept (formerly the chantry of St. Andrew) stands the tomb chest of Sir Thomas Markenfield (d. 1497) and his wife Eleanor Conyers. Sir Thomas was a retainer of Richard's, and later a Knight of the Body and Sheriff of Yorkshire, and was at Bosworth with Richard. Also in the north transept is the alabaster effigy of Sir Thomas Markenfield (d. 1398), who acquired the Lordship of Carlton Miniott (Thirsk) through marriage, bearing a stag on his livery collar, denoting service to Richard II.

The cathedral library includes portraits of Elizabeth Woodville and Elizabeth of York and a Ricardian banner commemorating Richard III's 550th birthday, donated by the Richard III Foundation in 2002. A copy of the Royal Collection portrait of Richard is now privately displayed in the offices of the Dean of Ripon.

Fountains Abbey [HG4 3DY]

Fountains Abbey was founded as an austere Cistercian community in the early C12th by expelled Benedictine monks of St Mary's Abbey, York. Fountains became wealthy from dairy and sheep farming and the wool industry.

In a letter to Cistercian abbots requesting donations for the building of Bernard's College, Oxford [now St. John's], Richard III praised Fountains for its obedience to its monastic rules. As well as giving offerings at shrines in the abbey, just after his son's death in May 1484, Richard granted Fountains a licence to dispose of lands within the Lordship of Middleham.

The abbey is in the care of the National Trust and open daily to visitors; admission charge.

Markenfield Hall [HG4 3AD]

With its licence to crenellate dated 1310, this picturesque mid-C14th manor house, built by the then architect of Ripon Minster, retains much of its medieval character and features, with a private chapel still in use and a vaulted undercroft ceiling in the utility-kitchen. It stands within a moated quadrangle courtyard, the drawbridge now replaced by a fixed bridge to the Tudor gatehouse. The family arms are depicted on a piscina in the chapel as well as on heraldic shields on the north side of the courtyard.

Sir Thomas Markenfield was one of Richard of Gloucester's Middleham retainers from 1471. He was on commissions of the peace to Somerset and was granted six manors there during 1484. He also received an annuity of 100 marks for life, possibly indicating his membership of the Council of the North. He became High Sheriff of Yorkshire in 1484 and a Knight of the Body to Richard III. He fought for Richard at Bosworth, and when he died in 1497 and he was buried in Ripon Cathedral.

His son, Sir Ninian, fought at Flodden Field, and his great-grandson was attainted for the Rising of the North, dying in poverty abroad. Forfeited to the Crown, the estate was bought by Fletcher Norton, ancestor to Lord Grantley, the present owner, and descendant of the Nortons, cousins of the Markenfields.

The Hall is still a family home and open only on selected afternoons during May/June (see website). Admission charge.

46. Skipton Castle & Holy Trinity Church

Skipton Castle [BD23 1AW]

Skipton Castle is considered one of the best preserved and complete medieval castles. Originating in the C12th the castle passed from Edward II to the Clifford family. John, 9th Lord Clifford, who had mercilessly killed Edmund Plantagenet (Richard III's brother) in cold blood after the Battle of Wakefield, died at the Battle of Ferrybridge (1461) and forfeited his estates.

Sir William Stanley was given the barony and estates in 1462, possibly for his support in Edward IV's victory at Towton in 1461. Lancastrian by birth, he supported York at Blore Heath (1459) and was made Lord Chamberlain after Towton. Stanley then surrendered Skipton to Richard of Gloucester in 1475 in exchange for Richard's castle in Chirk on the Welsh Marches.

The Honour of Skipton included extensive parklands and forest and the patronage of Bolton Priory. Richard is known to have visited Skipton on several occasions, and also purchased the manor of

Carleton-in-Craven, two miles south of Skipton, from William Singleton in 1480. The Honour of Skipton was returned to the Clifford family in 1485 when the Tudor manor house elements were added to the castle.

Skipton Castle is in private ownership and open daily 10-5pm (Sun 11-4pm); admission charge.

Holy Trinity Church, Skipton [BD23 1NJ]

Richard III patronised Holy Trinity Church, Skipton with a grant of £20 in 1483 to extend the building eastwards and construct its oak roof and roof bosses, which are still extant.

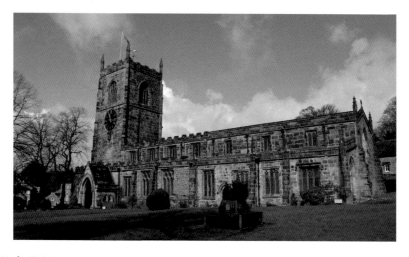

Holy Trinity is open to visitors during daylight hours.

47. Scotton & Knaresborough

Scotton [HG5 9HU]

Although related to the Percys of Northumberland, Sir Robert Percy of Scotton near Knaresborough (c.1445-85) was a stout Yorkist whose father, also Robert Percy, was taken prisoner at the Battle of Wakefield. The young Robert was subsequently raised in the household of Richard Neville, Earl of Warwick, probably at Middleham where it is likely he first met Richard of Gloucester and also Warwick's ward, Francis Lovell. He possibly fought with Richard at Barnet and in his Scottish campaigns, and was knighted on the eve of Richard's coronation at which he was prominent as Master of the Hall, serving the King and Queen at the feast. He was Escheator of Yorkshire in 1476, Comptroller of the Nottingham Castle household, and one of Richard's most loyal councillors, being created Captain of the Knights of the Body. Granted lands and manors for his service in the October rebellion of 1483 (including the formerly Stanley-owned Scotton), Percy died fighting for Richard at Bosworth. His son Robert fought for the Yorkists at the Battle of Stoke (1487), after which he was attainted but given pardon and restitution two years later.

One John Pullein of Scotton (d.1519) was sergeant of the kitchen to Richard III. By the early C17th Scotton was famous as the home village of Guy Fawkes.

Knaresborough [HG5 0EX]

As Steward of the Duchy of Lancaster's estates, Richard of Gloucester possessed the forest of Knaresborough. In 1483 and the year following, forest tenants were quarrelling with Fountains Abbey as to the rights of land boundaries between the two, a matter mediated by local retainers of Richard. In a letter of March 1485 Richard ordered that income from the estates at Knaresborough be assigned to pay for the 100 priests *'now being of our foundacion'* [of his collegiate chantry at York Minster]. As <u>Scotton</u> and Knaresborough Castle were a key focus of the Duchy of Lancaster Lordship, there was frequent conflict between Richard of Gloucester and the Percys who also maintained lordship of local lands, with possible disputes concerning the diverted affiliation of Percy retainers.

Richard owned a horse from the area – *'the little Whit[e] of Knaresborough'*.

Plumpton nearby [approx. HG5 8NA] was the home of Sir William Plumpton (1401-80) and his son, Sir Robert Plumpton (1453-1525) the principal recipients of the 'Plumpton Correspondence' - a collection of letters covering the period 1480-1510 which record the social and legal details of the family's life, and were received from men of law and business as well as the nobility, royalty and those in holy orders. Sir William fought for Lancaster at Towton (1461) where his son William died. Plumpton was later pardoned by Edward IV and regained his offices in 1471. His son Sir Robert was knighted by Richard of Gloucester near Berwick in 1482 when following his master, the Earl of Northumberland, and fought for Richard at Bosworth.

48.   St Martin's Church, Allerton Mauleverer [HG5 0SE]

Richard Mauleverer founded St Martin's Priory c.1100 nearby and a medieval church was built on this site in the late C12th, but the present one was rebuilt in the mid-C18th and passed to the Churches Conservation Trust in 1971. A fish-pond in the medieval park indicating a square moated site may mark the location of the earlier manor and vanished medieval village, where an C18th manor now stands.

In the north transept chapel of St Martin's Church are two wooden effigies of mid-C13th knights and a brass of Sir John (d. 1400) and

Eleanor Mauleverer. Here also are the alabaster effigies of Sir John Mauleverer (d. 1475) and Alyson Banks.

Sir John Mauleverer fought for the Lancastrians at Wakefield (1460), where he was created Knight Banneret, and subsequently fought at Towton. He joined John Neville's campaign for the Yorkists in 1464 and attended Edward IV's Treaty of Picquiny expedition to France in 1475.

His son, Sir Thomas (alongside Thomas's brothers Halnath and Robert) fought for Richard of Gloucester in the Scots campaign 1481/2, and also at the Battle of Bosworth. He conspired and rebelled against Henry VII, fighting again in 1487 for the Yorkist cause at the Battle of Stoke. He died before 1495.

After the October Rebellion of 1483, Richard III replaced southern officials who had rebelled and William Mauleverer became Escheator in Kent. Halnath Mauleverer - Sir Thomas' brother - who was one of the ushers of the king's chamber, became Sheriff of Devon and Master of the Game in the king's parks of Colcombe and Okehampton. The following November he was succeeded by Sir Thomas who was also given the castle and manor of Plympton in Devon.

The church is open to visitors during daylight hours.

49.   Cock Lodge, Topcliffe [YO7 3JL]

Civil unrest over Henry VII's heavy taxation began at Ayton in Cleveland in late April 1489, under the leadership of yeoman John Chambre. On 28 April 700 men confronted and killed Henry Percy, 4th Earl of Northumberland at Cock Lodge manor in the Earl's park just south-east of Topcliffe, near Thirsk. The Cleveland insurgents then joined forces with Sir John, Lord Egremont, a disinherited younger son of the Percy family, who had served Richard III as a Knight of the Body and in the October Rebellion. With nearly 5000 rebels from the North and East Ridings, they advanced to Doncaster before falling back to the city of York, being dispersed by the approach of Henry VII's armed guard. Egremont escaped to Margaret of Burgundy in Mechelen, Belgium, and John Chambre was tried and hanged. Henry Percy, 4th Earl of Northumberland is buried in Beverley Minster.

Whilst Thirsk tradition holds that Percy was dragged to his murder by the Great Elm on the Little Green, north of Thirsk marketplace, more contemporary accounts place the incident at Cock Lodge. The now vanished manor, the ancient Percy seat prior to Alnwick, and its motte-and-bailey earthworks are located close to the current Manor Farm, west of the Cod Beck, and in the fields on the east side of the A168.

50. Upsall Castle & St Wilfrid's Church, South Kilvington

Upsall Castle [YO7 2QJ]

Upsall Castle was begun by Geoffrey le Scrope c. 1327 near the village of South Kilvington but was demolished in the Civil War and rebuilt in the C19th. Some stonework of the southeast tower remains along with window heads showing the Scrope arms.

During the later Wars of the Roses the castle belonged to Thomas, 6th Baron Scrope of Upsall and Masham, cousin of John, Lord Scrope of Castle Bolton. Thomas was indentured as a young man into the household of Richard of Gloucester, and in 1477 married Elizabeth Neville, daughter of John Neville, Marquis Montagu, Richard's cousin.

Sir Thomas was a Commissioner of Array in Richard of Gloucester's Scottish campaign and knighted by him in 1481. He was a cupbearer at Richard's coronation, and he and his cousin John fought at Bosworth alongside Richard and also supported the claim of 'Lambert Simnel' in 1487. Imprisoned in the Tower, he was later released, fined and forbidden to live further than 22 miles from London. He died in 1493, aged 33.

St Wilfrid's Church, South Kilvington [YO7 2NN]

St Wilfrid's boasts Norman and Romanesque details, fragments of medieval glass and an inscribed black marble hexagonal font, originally created for Sir Thomas Scrope, 5th Baron Scrope of Masham (1428-75).

The inscription around the base reads - **'Dñs Thom[a]s le Scrōp et Elizabeth uxor ejus'**. The font may have originally stood in the chapel at Upsall Castle.

The church is open to visitors during daylight hours.

51.   Helmsley & Pickering

Helmsley Castle [YO62 5AB]

This C12th/C13th castle was originally in the possession of the de Roos Lords until the Battle of Hexham (1464) when Lancastrian leader Thomas, 9th Baron de Roos, was captured and beheaded in Newcastle and his son Edmund disinherited. Thomas' eldest daughter, Eleanor, married Sir Robert Manners of Etal Castle (Northumberland) c. 1465. Sir Robert was an MP and retainer of Richard of Gloucester. He was Sheriff of Northumberland in 1463, 1465 and 1485, Admiral of England and knighted by Richard in 1485. He fought with Richard at Bosworth. Sir Robert's son, George (b.1470) married Anne St Leger, Richard's niece by his sister Anne of York who had died in childbirth in 1476.

Edward IV officially granted the Helmsley estate to his brother George of Clarence in 1465, and upon George's execution in 1478 Richard purchased Helmsley and its surrounding parkland from the de Roos-Manners. The castle probably remained the home of the dowager baronesses and the new de Roos-Manners family, making it unlikely that Richard used Helmsley as a personal residence although he gained the support of local families and one Henry Pulley of Helmsley, eventually a Yeoman of the Crown, advanced in Richard's affinity in the years following. Richard visited the area in mid-May 1484 when he stayed at nearby Rievaulx Abbey.

English Heritage: open daily April-Oct (Sat/Sun only Nov-Mar); admission charge.

Pickering Castle [YO18 7AX]

Built between C12th and C14th, Pickering Castle had investment and visits from Henry II, Richard I, King John and Edwards I, II and III. Richard II was briefly held prisoner here. The castle became part of the Duchy of Lancaster in the C14th and played no part in the Wars of the Roses. In 1460 Edward IV established a chantry dedicated to the Virgin Mary in the castle chapel. In 1465 Richard of Gloucester was granted the Duchy of Lancaster Lordship of Pickering but appears to have had no direct influence there, as its officers remained unchanged.

In the early 1470s the stewardship of Pickering was shared between Richard of Gloucester and William, Lord Hastings. The Duchy Lordship extended from just south of Whitby to Filey Brigg, incorporating <u>Scarborough</u>. When strengthening Scarborough harbour port against the Scots, Richard ordered the use of 300 oak trees from the royal forest at Pickering. Sir Edmund Hastings of Pickering was on Richard's ducal council and was knighted by him on the Scottish campaign of 1482.

English Heritage: open daily from April-Oct (closed winter months); admission charge.

St Peter & St Paul's Church, Pickering [YO18 7BE]

This C12th church acquired in the C15th its two-storey south chapel, nave clerestory and embattled parapets, and is principally remarkable for its extensive nave wall paintings possibly following the medieval liturgical calendar and dating from the 1460s. The paintings depict Saints George and Christopher, Herod's feast with

Salome, the Coronation of the Virgin Mary and the Martyrdoms of St Edmund and St Thomas of Canterbury. Other paintings variously show the life of St Catherine of Alexandria, the burial and Assumption of Mary into Heaven, scenes from the Passion of Christ and the Seven Corporal Acts of Mercy.

St Peter & St Paul's is open to visitors during daylight hours.

52. Sheriff Hutton [YO60 6SX]

Sheriff Hutton Castle [YO60 6TA]

The remains of the motte-and-bailey castle, built by Bertram de Bulmer, Sheriff of York in the mid-C12th, are to the south of St Helen's churchyard. The stone castle at the west of the village was built by John, Lord Neville in the late C14th and passed to Ralph Neville, 1st Earl of Westmorland. Sheriff Hutton was held by the Beaufort Nevilles until the death of Richard Neville, Earl of Warwick in 1471 when the estates were given to Richard, Duke of Gloucester. Its convenient proximity to York may have contributed to its status as the headquarters (shared with Sandal Castle, Wakefield) of the Council of the North. The Council was established in 1484 as an effective government of the North of England for more than 150 years. As such, Richard and his retainers would have stayed regularly at Sheriff Hutton and the Court of Pleas met here to dispense justice based on common law. Over its gatehouse are four shields including the royal arms and the Neville saltire.

In October 1480, Richard received news at Sheriff Hutton of Scots insurgency, and in 1484 he established a royal household here for the young Edward of Warwick, son of George of Clarence, and another of Richard's nephews, John, Earl of Lincoln. John, Earl of Lincoln, was President of the Council of the North from 1483. An ordinance of July 1484 regulating the King's Household in the North mentions breakfast and livery provided for 'children' at Sheriff Hutton. Until his captaincy of Calais in Nov 1484 John of Gloucester, Richard's illegitimate son, may also have been resident at Sheriff Hutton. Richard's illegitimate daughter Katherine was married by May 1484, although she may previously have lived at Sheriff Hutton.

Anthony, Lord Rivers, was imprisoned here for 57 days during the Protectorate, at which time Richard added £10 to the salary of the chantry priest of 'Our Lady Chapel'. Elizabeth of York, the eldest daughter of Edward IV and sister to the former Edward V, was at Sheriff Hutton in 1485, possibly accompanied by one of her four sisters.

The castle is privately owned and is not open to visitors.

St Helen & the Holy Cross Church, Sheriff Hutton

This early C12th church is the burial site of George Neville, Duke of Bedford, the son of John Neville, who died in May 1483 aged 22, and of Sir Thomas Gower, Constable of Sheriff Hutton Castle, with his wife. Four chantry chapels were built in the church in the C15th for the local manor-holding families: Nevilles, Gowers, Wythams and Dacres. Edward IV's 'sun in splendour' and Neville and Dacre shields feature in the fragments of medieval stained glass.

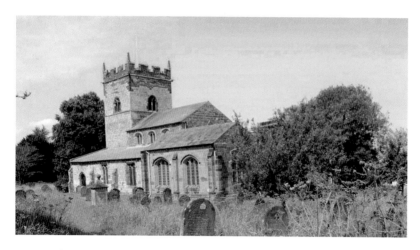

A worn alabaster effigy of a child in the north chapelry has for many years been identified as Edward of Middleham, Prince of Wales, and Richard and Anne's only child. However, there is no record of Edward's burial here and the early C15th style, the ambiguity of armorial bearings in the church, poor quality alabaster and the unlikelihood of a royal burial in a village church, suggest it is unlikely to be the tomb of Edward. After news of Edward's death in late April 1484 there is no account of Richard's visiting Sheriff Hutton until 24 May.

The effigy is dressed in early C15th pleated robes with a cap of maintenance on its head. The tomb chest depicts the Holy Trinity, and a kneeling suppliant (the child's father?) in armour, praying aloud and flanked by angels. The west end panel shows the cross of St George. The tomb is not mentioned in a Visitation account of 1584, and possibly originally stood in the chapel at Sheriff Hutton Castle which included a chantry of the Holy Trinity and Our Lady. The tomb may have been for one of the four sons of Ralph Neville, 1st Earl of Westmorland and Joan Beaufort, who died young.

The church is open to visitors during daylight hours.

53. Scarborough & Scarborough Castle

King Richard III House [YO11 1PE] - Parts of this three-storey stone building date to the C15th. Scarborough shipbuilder, Thomas Sage, who may have owned the property, received payment of £40 on 28 May 1484 from Richard III. Whilst Richard could have stayed here in May 1484 commissioning provisions and naval preparations for the *'works at Dunbar'* (English garrisons besieged by the Scots), his commissions were officially sent from the castle.

A first floor room is named the King's Hall and on the second floor the 'King's Bedchamber' has elaborate plasterwork on the ceiling dating from 1600 featuring the York Rose, heraldic badge of Richard's family, and the bull of the Nevilles (for Richard's wife Anne). In the later C20th a grotesque stone carving of Richard with crooked back, cloven feet and chained body stood outside, protected by an iron grill. The figure was stolen c. 2000.

Town – Richard, Duke of Gloucester first campaigned here with a fleet against Scotland in 1471/72 and in 1474 (in exchange for Chesterfield, Bushey and Ware) he acquired from Edward IV the Lordships of Falsgrave, Scarborough Castle and Northstead Manor.

Richard's especial patronage is shown in a vellum charter of spring 1485 (in Scarborough Art Gallery), creating Scarborough as a 'shire incorporate', an honour shared only with London, Bristol and Norwich, entitling it to a Sheriff and a Mayor responsible for the north-east coast, and an export opportunity for Yorkshire's vast wool economy. It states: *'The special Affection which we have and bear towards the Town of Scardeburgh [...] and in consideration of their good and faithful Behavior and for their more secure Immunity and quiet and also for other Causes...'* The charter was invalidated by Henry VII.

Richard developed the harbour as Lord High Admiral and King, with 300 oaks from Pickering to buttress the ruined quay and create a bulwark on Sandside. By 1534 this sea-wall was *'yn ruine by the se rage'*. He also re-built the town gateways at Newborough [YO11 1ET] and Oldborough [YO11 1XE] Bars, but a wall of squared stone between them was never completed. A short surviving length of wall on Sandside bears a Civic Society blue plaque to Richard.

As king, Richard reduced the town's 'rent' by £10 a year and insisted that £42 11s of the remainder go to King's Hall (now Trinity College) Cambridge. Scarborough Town Hall still pays Trinity College £42.55 every year.

Castle [YO11 1HY] - Richard was here on 22 May 1484 and re-visited to muster a fleet against Henry Tudor from 27 June to 11 July, accompanied by his wife, Anne. Little remains of the Queen's Tower where she stayed but the impressive gateway, mid-C12th keep and aspects of North and South Bays invite a visit. Richard was the last monarch to stay in the castle.

English Heritage: open daily Apr-Oct (Sat/Sun only Nov-Jan; see website for Feb); admission charge

LINKS:

Northern Dales RIII Group on Facebook -
https://www.facebook.com/Northern-Dales-Richard-III-Group-
1555111188072365/ A group meeting monthly for those interested
in Richard III and the C15th Northern Dales; based in Teesdale.

Richard III: Rumour & Reality - http://richardiii-ipup.org.uk/ York
University's website on Richard's history in and legacy to the North.

Richard III Society - http://www.richardiii.net/ The oldest Ricardian
society, from 1924, promoting research into his life and times.

Yorkshire Branch (Richard III Society) -
http://www.richardiiiyorkshire.org/yorkshirebranch.html The
oldest Richard III Society branch founded 1960; study days,
commemorations and visits.

Richard III Society (US branch) - http://www.r3.org/ Additional
background, information and key texts on Ricardian matters.

The Society of Friends of King Richard III -
http://www.silverboar.org/ A York-based society formed in 1978
to promote Richard in the North, especially in the city of York.

Richard III Foundation
https://www.facebook.com/richardIIIFoundation/ An educational
body focusing on Richard and the Wars of the Roses with an annual
conference.

Richard III's Loyal Supporters
https://www.r3loyalsupporters.org/index.html An international
Society which aims to counter Ricardian myths and untruths with a
more positive view of Richard as a man and as a king.

INDEX

Allerton Mauleverer 92
Appleby 39, 40, 42
Askrigg 66, 67, 77
Aysgarth 67, 68, 77
Barnard Castle 9, 11, 13, 14, 18, 19, 21, 27, 54, 79
Bearpark 32, 33
Bedale 61, 79, 80
Bewcastle 41, 49
Bowes Castle 20
Brancepeth 24, 25, 28, 30, 31
Brougham 42, 43
Carlisle 41, 42, 47, 48, 49
Castle Bolton..50, 53, 58, 59, 64, 65, 66, 82, 94
Catterick 60
Chester-le-Street 35, 36
Cotherstone 19
Coverham 70, 71, 72
Croft-on-Tees 50
Croxdale Hall 28
Durham .. 11, 13, 14, 18, 20, 22, 23, 24, 25, 26,
      28, 29, 30, 31, 32, 33, 34, 35, 36, 38, 47, 50,
      54, 55, 56, 64, 71, 83
Easby Abbey 18, 59, 69
Egglestone Abbey 17, 18, 19, 20, 59
Fountains Abbey 76, 87, 91
Gainford 13, 22, 23
Gilling West 53, 54
Great Musgrave 41
Helmsley 95, 96
Hexham 22, 37, 38, 65, 95
Hornby 27, 55, 62, 63, 64, 73
Jervaulx Abbey 32, 52, 68, 76, 77, 81, 84
Kendal 40, 45, 53, 63
Knaresborough 91, 92
Low Butterby 28

Lumley Castle 36, 37
Markenfield 86, 87, 88
Marrick Priory 57, 58
Masham 23, 54, 82, 83, 94, 95
Middleham .. 11, 13, 14, 16, 18, 21, 25, 50, 55,
      58, 61, 62, 66, 71, 72, 73, 74, 75, 76, 77, 78,
      79, 81, 82, 86, 87, 88, 91, 100
Nappa Hall 66, 67, 68
Norton Conyers 85
Penrith 41, 42, 43
Pickering 60, 96, 97, 102
Raby Castle 25, 27
Ravensworth   19, 20, 46, 52, 53, 54, 78, 79, 84
Richmond 13, 20, 54, 57, 58, 59, 60, 62, 66, 77,
      79, 83
Ripon 85, 86, 87
Scarborough 11, 35, 36, 97, 101, 102
Scotton 91, 92
Sedbury 53
Shap Abbey 43, 44
Sheriff Hutton 11, 98, 99, 100
Simonburn 38
Skipton 41, 43, 89, 90
Snape Castle 81
South Cowton 20, 55, 56
South Kilvington 94, 95
Staindrop 23
Topcliffe 93
Tudhoe 28
Upsall Castle 94, 95
Walworth Castle 23
Wath 85
Wensley 59, 69
West Tanfield 84
Wetheral 2
Witton Castle 27, 28